"As a mental wellness advocate who wrote a book about my mental health journey, I adore proven methods and practices that help people deal with trauma, pain, and struggles. Bravo for Dr. Christopher Cortman on his new book, *The Guided Imagery Cure*. The stories are inspiring and a testament to how taking care of both body and mind can change your life for the better."

—**Nita Sweeney**, author of *Depression Hates a Moving Target*

"*The Guided Imagery Cure* offers an in-depth and encouraging look, including specific examples, at how imagery can help a person overcome traumatic experiences. Dr. Cortman shows how these experiences can even become something one can grow from and gain a sense of control over with the skillful use of guided imagery. He invites us to envision a world where what can be first held in the mind's eye can manifest in tangible reality. This simple and profound tool can help individuals and clinicians alike to deal with very complex issues. This book will teach you how to use guided imagery to great effect."

—**Lynda Monk**, MSW, RSW, CPCC, director of International Association for Journal Writing

Praise for *The Guided Imagery Cure*

"Dr. Christopher Cortman has written a book on the power of guided imagery that deserves wide readership. Guided imagery can ever so gently release a person from whatever trauma has claimed their mind at any time in the past. Cortman explains its use and effectiveness in such simple language. The healing can begin immediately. It's definitely a must-read for both practitioners and sufferers alike. The world will be made better by this book."

—**Karen Casey**, PhD, author of bestselling *Each Day a New Beginning*

"Guided imagery is popular. World-class athletes use it to visualize success. Cancer patients use it to visualize healing. Guided imagery has a thousand uses. But did you know just how powerful a tool it can be? Learn all about the tremendous, life-changing value of visualizing in Christopher Cortman's excellent *The Guided Imagery Cure*. Highly recommended!"

—**Eric Maisel**, PhD, author of *Redesign Your Mind*

"As someone who works with first responders, veterans, nurses, and others deeply impacted by trauma, I wholeheartedly endorse Dr. Chris Cortman's book, *The Guided Imagery Cure*. I regularly witness the costly and devastating toll of unresolved trauma and grief, and I see how desperate people are for help. I believe *The Guided Imagery Cure* can serve as a powerful healing tool and I will be recommending this book to every person I encounter who suffers from invisible wounds."

—**Kim Colegrove**, author of *Mindfulness for Warriors* and *Wellness Warrior Style*

"While in practice as a therapist, the clients with whom I used guided imagery often experienced wonderful, and sometimes amazing, results. I still use imagery to help soothe and transform my personal pain. Because I know from experience that imagery is an effective cure, I am thrilled to know that a book as wise, practical, and compassionate as *The Guided Imagery Cure* is now available to everyone. I strongly encourage you to give yourself the gift of exploring this book."

—**Sue Patton Thoele**, author of *The Courage to Be Yourself* and *How to Stay Upbeat in a Beat Down World*

"If you or someone you love has been suffering from trauma of any kind—whether it's fresh or long-frozen—this book is for you! Guided imagery offers a powerful and innovative way to navigate the hard parts of life we may have thought we'd struggle with forever. However, we learn from our expert author that we can use our imagination to 'confront trauma face-to-face and then put it away.' Through compelling stories and examples, he shares how people of all ages and backgrounds have been able to release painful or debilitating trauma and find new freedom and joy. With compassion, expertise, and care, Dr. Cortman serves as a trusted guide, helping readers discover their own path to healing through guided imagery."

—**Sherry Richert Belul**, founder of Simply Celebrate and author of *Say It Now* and *The Love List of a Lifetime*

THE
GUIDED
IMAGERY
CURE

Books by the Author

Your Mind: An Owner's Manual for a Better Life

Take Control of Your Anxiety: A Drug-Free Approach to Living a Happy, Healthy Life

Keep Pain in the Past: Getting over Trauma, Grief and the Worst That's Ever Happened to You

The Social Black Belt

Praying for the Darkness

THE
GUIDED
IMAGERY
CURE

The Best Proven Methods for Quickly
Resolving and Healing Trauma

Dr. Christopher Cortman

Books That Save Lives

For trade and wholesale sales, please contact Ingram Publisher Services at customer.service@ingramcontent.com or +1.800.509.4887.

The Guided Imagery Cure: The Best Proven Methods for Quickly Resolving and Healing Trauma

Library of Congress Cataloging-in-Publication number: 2025931390
ISBN: (print) 978-1-68481-750-4, (ebook) 978-1-68481-751-1
BISAC category code: SEL043000 SELF-HELP / Post-Traumatic Stress Disorder (PTSD)

To those who, standing in the ruins of their lives,
discovered rebirth through the transformative
power of imagery.

Table of Contents

Introduction

Years ago, I found myself intrigued by my then-partner's fascination with *The Long Island Medium*. For those unfamiliar, the show featured Theresa Caputo, a charismatic woman with an unmistakable Long Island accent and a towering blonde hairdo, who claimed to communicate with the departed.

While skeptics might question the authenticity of such "reality" shows, I couldn't help but notice something profound: the impact of Caputo's readings on her audience. Whether she was truly communicating with spirits or not became almost irrelevant in the face of the profound relief and hope she offered grieving individuals.

Picture this: A woman, burdened by guilt, asks if her late father has forgiven her for accidentally burning down his house. Caputo, with unwavering confidence, assures her that he's at peace and has indeed forgiven her. The woman's tears of relief speak volumes about the weight lifted from her shoulders.

One after another, people sought answers from Caputo. "Is my daughter okay?" "Is my mother still suffering?" "Does my late husband blame me for his death?" With each response, Caputo wielded the power to allay their deepest fears and offer much-needed closure.

Reality or not, I've encountered numerous individuals who've had similar experiences with mediums, hearing exactly what they needed to heal from their loss. This phenomenon points to a crucial truth: there is tremendous healing available to those suffering from grief, trauma, and loss.

Sometimes, this healing comes from accepting the words of a trusted source—be it a medium, a religious leader, a parent, a friend, or a mental health professional. Other times, people need to experience something more visceral, often in the form of visualization, to achieve that closure.

This is where guided imagery comes into play. When used properly, this technique can work a special kind of magic, providing closure and healing to a myriad of sufferers, often in just one session.

Let me share a story from early in my career as a licensed psychologist (which I elaborate on in my book *Keep Pain in the Past*). I received an urgent call from the local fire chief, pleading for help. His friend, a police officer trainee, was on the brink of suicide following a training accident in which he was shot in the face with a blank. Though physically recovered, he was trapped in a cycle of nightmares, reliving the trauma night after night.

Faced with this critical situation, I turned to a technique I'd learned about in graduate school: guided imagery.

This age-old, theoretically simple tool has the potential to help patients revisit unfinished issues in their lives and finally achieve closure.

In a single session, I guided "Dave" through a visualization where he imagined watching his trauma on a movie screen, then entering the scene to comfort his past self. The results were nothing short of remarkable. Dave reported that the disturbing dream occurred only once more that night and never again. Years later, when he returned for help with marital issues, he confirmed, "Doc, we put that away years ago with that imagery thing we did."

Since that success with Dave, I've used guided imagery more than a hundred times, consistently achieving remarkable results. With thirty-nine years of post-license experience and over eighty thousand hours of psychotherapy under my belt, I can confidently say that no technique is as effective in providing healing and closure in a single session as guided imagery.

This book aims to shed light on this powerful tool that's been hiding in plain sight since before the advent of modern psychology. My hope is that by sharing this knowledge, we can offer immediate understanding and resurrect a valuable technique to help those suffering from trauma, grief, and loss.

As we embark on this journey together, prepare to discover the transformative power of your own mind. Whether you're a mental health professional looking to expand your toolkit, or someone seeking personal healing, the pages that follow will open your eyes to the incredible potential of guided imagery.

Welcome to a world where healing is just a visualization away.

Chapter One

What Is Guided Imagery?

Remember *Wide World of Sports* on Saturday afternoons? Each episode began with the same introduction: "Spanning the globe to bring you the constant variety of sport. The thrill of victory...and the agony of defeat."

While the "thrill of victory" showed jubilant Little Leaguers, the "agony of defeat" was forever immortalized by Slovenian ski jumper Vinko Bogataj's spectacular crash. Week after week, viewers witnessed Bogataj's tumble in slow motion, his athletic low point broadcast in living color.

Thankfully, most of us don't have to watch our worst moments on television every weekend. Yet, for those grappling with trauma, Bogataj's experience might feel painfully familiar. One of the hallmarks of post-traumatic stress disorder (PTSD) is the intrusive replay of traumatic memories through flashbacks and nightmares—a personal highlight reel of life's worst moments.

Why Does This Happen?

Think of the mind as a stomach: anything not properly digested may repeat on you. Just as you might taste this afternoon's egg salad hours later, unprocessed traumatic experiences can linger, sometimes indefinitely. While that spicy pizza from third grade is long forgotten, if the class bully had thrown it in your face, you might still be tasting it today.

But here's the good news: if you're haunted by such traumas, they're treatable—even curable—immediately. Unlike poor Bogataj, you don't have to watch yourself crash indefinitely. Let me illustrate with two true stories about people who were crashing down their own mental mountains until they encountered a technique called guided imagery.

Stafford's Story: The Vietnam Helicopter Crash

Stafford's "mountain fall" occurred fifty years ago, while serving in Vietnam. While in the demilitarized zone one day, Stafford witnessed a helicopter landing with four soldiers to refuel their aircraft. Moments later, the helicopter flipped over and caught fire, exploding into an overwhelming inferno that devoured the soldiers instantly. Stafford and his men watched helplessly, horrified at the tragedy, wondering what they could do to challenge the impenetrable wall of fire. But there wasn't anything they could do. Stafford and his soldiers said little to each other because they were trained to move on after losses. They never stopped long enough to process the horror show that they had witnessed, just one of several such episodes in the combat soldier's experience of war.

So here we are fifty years later, and Stafford can still experience the scene as if it had happened last night, from the wall of fire to feeling impotent and helpless—even the pungent smell of burning flesh. All of these emotional and sensory experiences repeat on Stafford, even though they occurred half a century ago.

After several months of treatment, Stafford was brave enough to share the story with me in the hope of finally putting the story to rest and freeing himself from the repetition of the horrible scene. He allowed me to facilitate a guided imagery technique with him wherein I had him relax, enter a movie theater in his mind, and then watch the incident one last time, in an effort to promote closure to the story, some semblance of healing. Below is Stafford's version of the trauma, followed by his guided imagery experience.

Stafford's Story

I was one of seven helicopter crew members in an assault-lift company. We were awaiting our turn to refuel at a remote, forward deployed, hot-refuel site. "Forward deployed" means that we were near enemy lines. "Hot-refuel" means lives in danger. When you're in active combat, there isn't any time to shut down and restart, so the engines keep running while the gas goes in. We were waiting to hover into one of the refueling pits. I was standing outside and to the rear of the helicopter. Part of my job was to ensure that someone didn't accidentally walk into the spinning tail rotor—standard procedure also known as "clear the rear."

As I looked up and back toward the refuel pits, to my horror I saw one aircraft hover backward out of the pit, then suddenly and violently spin right and flip upside down, exploding into a fireball. One guy, the left door gunner/crew chief, was thrown from the aircraft. But three others, two pilots and the right side door gunner, were trapped in the inferno. I screamed an alarm over my helmet microphone, then ran toward the burning aircraft about a hundred yards away.

Unfortunately, the heat was too intense for me to get close, and I had to retreat. I still cannot describe the absolute horror and brutality of the raging fire, mercilessly consuming the poor men trapped inside. On the one hand, the intellectual part of my mind knew that I could not change reality, and that I was not responsible for their enormous suffering and violent death. On the other hand, the emotional part of my mind couldn't help but feel guilty, in spite of the helplessness. I wanted to change it so much. They burned alive.

Stafford's Imagery

What I envisioned was as clear as the front row seat at an IMAX theater. My vantage point was at the back of a small group of people gathered tightly at the base of a small, grassy knoll to our front. I saw a sky in magnificent royal blue, like that of an afternoon summer storm. I remember thick, rich green grass everywhere swaying from a refreshing, cool wind that seemed to awaken my senses. The vista and sensations were suddenly replaced with the undeniable sound of Huey helicopter rotors and turbine engine sounds approaching from the distance. There was a noticeable stirring in the crowd. Excitement rippled through my soul. Vietnam-era combat soldiers are infinitely familiar with the unique sense of excitement and relief stimulated by these sounds, which generally denoted imminent rescue, fire support, or the arrival of badly needed resources.

As the Huey rapidly approached into view of our crowd, it was a clean, brilliant white in color, without the typical armament or weapons systems of that period and, astonishingly, the pilots were not men. They were angels, with the wings and robes and imagery that portray angels in paintings and the media.

The aircraft gently set down on top of the grassy knoll to the crowd's front and the aft cabin door purposefully slid open, allowing the crew chief (yes, an angel also) to step out and with a "come here" gesture, motioned to the crowd to come forward. Suddenly three figures from the front of the crowd, obscured until now, stepped forward and began walking up the gently sloped hill toward the awaiting aircraft. The intended passengers were patting one another on the back and looking back to the remaining crowd with smiles and visible tears.

The excitement seemed to build with the rapid increase in rotor speed and sounds as the three passengers climbed into the aircraft cabin. The crew chief climbed aboard, and as the cabin door slowly slid closed, the passengers presented one final wave goodbye to the crowd before disappearing inside.

> Then, with a graceful, but purposeful movement, the
> aircraft lifted from the ground, hesitated in a stable
> hover for a moment, then, in seamless maneuver,
> executed a sharp right turn and rapidly climbed into
> the heavens.

As you can see, Stafford created his own conclusion to a horrible incident. The angelic rescue wasn't part of the original traumatic event—Stafford added this element during the guided imagery session.

This is the power of imagery: what your mind sees, your nervous system processes as real. You've experienced this if you've ever woken up in tears from a painful dream. The question is: can we harness this power for healing?

In Stafford's case, the answer was a resounding yes. His unconscious mind finally found closure for a trauma that had haunted him for over five decades. Remarkably, he provided the ending himself.

Todd's Story: The Tragic Accident

Some readers might object that Stafford's trauma was over fifty years old and had almost healed anyway. There is an adage which says, "Time heals all wounds." Not so. Consider the story of Todd.

Approximately six years ago, Todd was leaving high school in his car. At an intersection along the way, a bicyclist suddenly pulled directly into Todd's path. Seconds later, Todd fatally struck the sixty-six-year old gentleman. The four other adults he was traveling with saw the traffic light change and obeyed the signal. But not this gentleman. He continued pedaling...directly into traffic. Todd's car went up and over the bicycle. Todd rushed to help, but could only observe the cyclist's last breath. He was dead within seconds. Todd, the cyclist's wife, and their friends felt helpless, devastated.

Seeing the young man overcome by helplessness, the cyclist's wife apologized to Todd. She knew it wasn't his fault—her husband had always been impatient, she said. She feared that Todd would carry the experience of striking and killing her husband for the rest of his life. Minutes later, Todd's parents arrived on the scene. In front of them and everyone, she asked Todd an unforgettable question: "Would you be my prayer partner, Todd?" Without ever knowing whether Todd or his family even believed in a supreme being, she wanted Todd as a teammate, a prayer pal.

As you might imagine, Todd was more than a little shaken that night. He thought about never driving to school again, maybe never driving at all. When he finally fell asleep, he dreamt about the cyclist, about the last breath.

Todd was relieved when his parents called me for an emergency appointment. Luckily, there was a three o'clock cancellation that day. Todd was seen twenty-four hours after the accident. We reviewed the symptoms of acute trauma: the intrusive memories of the accident, the potential flashbacks and nightmares, a tendency to avoid reminders of the accident (like driving), the exaggerated startle response, the hypervigilance (extreme caution), and the inability to relax and feel well in his own skin. I also told Todd that he might start keeping more to himself, just hanging out in his room, preferring solitary activities like video games to buddies and young ladies. I cautioned him that, if nothing was done, he might withdraw more and more from the life he once knew.

Todd told me that he already knew this, as his cousin had been involved in a fatal car accident the previous year. Now he was holed up in his room, drinking all day, hiding from the world.

I asked Todd about faith, about whether he believed in an afterlife, and where the cyclist might be at this time. He claimed (in front of his parents) that, although he was not an active churchgoer, he believed in God, Jesus, and an afterlife. He liked the idea that the cyclist was in heaven. After all, his wife had indicated that her husband was "a good, God-fearing man."

I decided to introduce Todd to the concept of guided imagery, and create a plan to address the accident proactively, rather than wait to see if he developed the abovementioned symptoms. Perhaps we could head this off at the pass, so to speak, and prevent a full-blown manifestation of the syndrome known as post-traumatic stress disorder (PTSD).

With his parents flanking him, Todd heard me describe the procedure: in his own mind, he'd watch a video of the accident, then imagine a face-to-face meeting between himself and the cyclist. This would hopefully provide some peace and bring closure to the trauma. I told him it might sound a bit quirky, and suggested that he talk to his parents about it, then relay a message back to my office.

But Todd didn't wait another moment. "I want to try your imagery thing." I figured he was hurting.

Exactly one week later, his stepmom brought him in. Within two minutes, she made it clear that she would trust "you boys" to get the job done. She left the room so Todd and I could get started. Todd closed his eyes.

I began to induce a relaxation response I will describe in greater detail later in the book. After approximately five minutes of relaxation, Todd selected a movie theater south of town, one he'd been to several times and felt at home in. Now, in imagination, I handed him a remote that afforded him control over the movie of the accident and encouraged him to watch the scene from beginning to end, one more time. "Finish the scene. You never have to go back there again. The cyclist is not there anymore."

I had him imagine that the projectionist came down to our seats (we were the only ones seated in this imaginary theater) and handed Todd a DVD of the accident. Straight away, we went outside behind the theater to the dumpster— every theater has a dumpster outback—to destroy the DVD and toss it out, never to be seen again.

Still in imagination, we arranged a meeting with the cyclist, to be held in a location of Todd's choosing. Ironically, he selected a bicycle motocross (BMX) park where he could pedal around furiously for a couple of laps while the newly deceased gentleman watched in amazement and amusement.

After Todd completed the course twice, he pulled his bicycle over to converse with the gentleman. I spoke for the latter, congratulating Todd on his remarkable BMX skills. I then had the gentleman explain to Todd:

> Thank you for meeting with me. You are one incredible bicyclist. If I could ride a bike like that, well, I guess I wouldn't be here. Listen, I want you to know that I have special permission to be here with you today, but only one time, given our circumstances. I want you to know that I am happy, very well actually, and at peace. I know I have no right to ask you for anything, but still, I have a couple of requests to make. First, I want to ask you to forgive me for my mistake. Please do not think of me in a negative or depressing way. I want you to know it was my mistake, and I am fine. Truthfully, I'd like to be a source of inspiration to you, someone rooting for you on the other side. Consider me a friend, if you will.
>
> I'd also like to ask you to honor my wife's request and say a prayer with her. I know it's a lot to ask of a young man to pray with an older lady, especially one you don't even know, but I think you might find it helpful in some way. Anyway, it's just a request, that's all. She's a wonderful woman, and it may be a great thing to have her in your corner. Besides, from what I'm learning in this new life, prayer is powerful and changes things. So, just a request...

Next, I had Todd respond to the gentleman, once again in
the silence of his own mind, allowing him a chance to say
anything he needed to convey: an apology, something about
the prayer with his wife, a commitment to think positively
about the accident and how maybe God brought them
together for His purposes, whatever. I did not ask Todd to
express his thoughts and feelings aloud—I don't know what
he said to the gentleman. I allotted him whatever time he
needed to speak his mind in the silence of my office. His
silence lasted about two minutes before he raised his right
index finger—a pre-arranged signal that he was ready to
proceed to the next step.

Immediately, I urged Todd to prepare to bid farewell to his
new friend. "Make sure you've told him everything you need
to say, and heard what you need to hear. When you have, give
me that right index finger one more time." Seconds later,
Todd complied once again.

I continued:

> Now, I'd like to ask you to prepare to say goodbye to the
> gentleman, it is time to let him return to the afterlife,
> where he will be living in a new dimension. Again, he'll
> be fine. And it's okay to release him and the accident
> scene, once and for all. Shake hands, hug, whatever
> you wanna do to bid farewell to him. Remember, it's
> okay to think of him, but in a positive way. The good
> Lord has used you as a vehicle to bring him to the next
> level, and all parties in this incident will be blessed by
> God. Ready to return to the office?

One more time, he raised his right index finger to indicate yes.

> I will count backward from five to zero now. When
> I reach zero, I will snap my fingers. Please open
> your eyes at that point, feeling refreshed, relieved,
> rejuvenated, and ready to take on the day...five, four,
> three, two, one...

Snap!

Todd opened his eyes and, as is true with almost all guided imagery clients, was remarkably quiet. "That was so real!" he said finally, but nothing else.

Even after conducting more than one hundred guided imagery sessions over my thirty-nine years of clinical experience, I wasn't prepared for what Todd shared during his third session. He was much different than previously, seemingly unburdened, probably the person he was before the accident. He was also excited—not so much to tell me that he had spoken to the gentleman's wife (he had), nor that he was driving to school (he was), or that he was sleeping through the night without nightmares and flashbacks (yes). No, Todd was excited because he had won first place in the BMX racing championships for the entire state of Florida! He had never accomplished that feat previously, so he was proud and overjoyed. He would have talked about it all session if allowed to, but I needed to interrupt his victory lap with my clinical questions: "Is the accident repeating in your mind? Does it interrupt your school day? Do you find yourself withdrawing into your own room? Are you more anxious than usual? How was your drive in to the office? Can you concentrate at school?"

Todd's answers were succinct. "After the imagery, I felt fine, like everything was going to be okay. I didn't know it would work like this, but I am better. Truthfully, I don't think I need to come back anymore."

For me, it was a very good sign that Todd felt that he had received what he needed and could return to normal. Given his remarkable progress, I asked him if I could tell his story for educational purposes. He did me one better. "I'm not the greatest at public speaking, but I would tell the story with you. I would be happy to have people hear about how the imagery thing helped me feel better. Just let me know, and I'll go on stage with you."

I followed up with Todd's family about six months later. I wanted to make sure all was well before including his story in this book. I called and spoke to his stepmother. Life was crazy, she said, but Todd was fine and would be willing to share his story with anyone. She was grateful to have her son back. Oh, and she made a new friend in the process—she reportedly talks to the gentleman's widow every week.

So, What Is Guided Imagery?

Is it a magic trick? A sleight-of-hand that fools you into believing your problems have vanished? Or perhaps a form of repression that makes you forget your trauma?

Actually, it's none of these. Guided imagery isn't magic, trickery, or induced forgetting. Instead, it's a method that allows you to confront your trauma face-to-face and then put it away. Rather than letting your trauma define your life, guided imagery helps you reduce its significance, weaving it into the fabric of your experience as something you can grow from.

Imagery puts you in control of the movie playing in your head. With it, you can finish the horror of combat, overcome a dog attack, process a car accident, heal from bullying or abuse, or address any other type of trauma. By controlling the visual, you can face your scariest monsters and release their power over you, achieving mastery over traumatic episodes once and for all.

But guided imagery's potential extends far beyond trauma resolution. As you'll discover in the following chapters, you can use this technique to reduce anxiety, resolve long-standing grief, improve athletic performance, or even overcome phobias. The applications are limitless, because visualizing something allows the mind to process it as reality.

Remember, what you see in your mind's eye, your nervous system processes as fact.[1] This is why dreams can have such a profound emotional impact, leaving you feeling terrified, angry, amused, anxious, or embarrassed upon waking. A dream is just a movie you wrote, directed, and starred in, but don't tell that to your nervous system—it feels the emotional impact as if it were real.

---

1 Ackerman, C. E. (2023, May 19). Guided imagery: How to and benefits of visualization techniques. PositivePsychology.com. positivepsychology.com/guided-imagery

The same principle applies to guided imagery. Just ask Stafford or Todd. Their experiences demonstrate the transformative power of this technique—a power that you, too, can harness for healing and personal growth.

As we delve deeper into the world of guided imagery in the coming chapters, prepare to discover how this simple yet profound technique can help you rewrite the narrative of your life, one visualization at a time.

Chapter Two

The Case for Guided Imagery: Time Does Not Heal All Wounds

I n this chapter, we'll explore the psychological foundations of guided imagery and its role in healing trauma. We'll delve into the concept of closure, the nature of trauma, and the psychological processes involved in healing. By understanding these elements, you'll gain insight into why guided imagery can be such a powerful tool for personal growth and recovery.

The Importance of Closure

In Chapter One, I described the use of guided imagery in two cases of traumatic stress. Both cases involved the use of imagination or fantasy to produce a particular kind of experience, which psychologists call "closure."

Recall that Stafford deeply wanted to change the outcome for the soldiers devoured by the inferno. Since this was impossible, the experience remained emotionally incomplete in his mind. Likewise, Todd knew that running over the cyclist was not his fault, and this was confirmed by the gentleman's wife. Nevertheless, Todd felt that the experience should not have happened as it did. Both Stafford and Todd were able to put their trauma in a better place by elaborating their experience in the context of their larger belief system, their faith in God, in order to reframe and bring closure to their experience.

Stafford imagined that the soldiers were taken up to heaven by angels. Todd met with the gentleman at a BMX course, and again, the gentleman was happy and doing just fine. The larger context of their beliefs allowed them to reframe the experience, thereby yielding emotional release and closure. No longer are Stafford and Todd preoccupied with their respective traumatic events. With their emotional power discharged, these events faded into the background. Stafford and Todd resumed their everyday lives, no longer carrying the burden of these traumas.

What Is Closure?

Let's explore this idea a little more deeply. I'll begin by staking the following claim: Obtaining closure is fundamental to psychological healing. Psychological issues that find closure are over, finished, kaput. Closure allows you to move on.

How do you know when you've achieved closure? The issue no longer interferes with your life. For instance, imagine that, one day, your apparently loving partner decides to end the relationship with no advance warning. You might find yourself plagued by insomnia, tossing and turning, and wondering exactly what happened. Closure here lays the foundation for accepting such a dramatic change of fortune in the relationship as it is. It may or may not answer the question "why." Maybe a relationship ends and you receive an encyclopedic explanation. Maybe your partner "Hops on the bus, Gus" (with appreciation to Paul Simon, *Fifty Ways to Leave Your Lover*), and there goes the "us."

Either way, closure is the realization and acceptance that:

1. The relationship is over, and

2. You will be okay.

Without internalizing both of these concepts, there is no closure. You will continue to be plagued by the psychological and physical symptoms that were born the day your partner left.

Back to Stafford and Todd: their traumatic events were completed by being reframed in the context of their spiritual belief system. Otherwise, their experiences would simply remain open, as Stafford's did for fifty years.

The Stream of Consciousness and Closure

You complete your life experiences in ways both big and small, without realizing it. Now let's talk about your moment-to-moment "stream of consciousness," that is, the sequence of thoughts running through your mind at any given moment. Each such thought evokes the next in the sequence, either continuing the current topic or finishing it.

For instance, let's say your mother's sister, Aunt Edna, died several years ago in a car accident. You were emotionally but not geographically close to Edna. You are sad about losing her, but not devastated. Edna's April birthday elicits a stream of associations, including:

- Aunt Edna's succulent apple pie
- Evenings spent with Aunt Edna and Uncle John playing Monopoly
- Aunt Edna's accident
- The funeral service
- The sadness that followed
- Finally, so many pleasant memories of Aunt Edna

Each association continued the topic of the stream—Aunt Edna—each thought being loosely bound to the one preceding it. Finally, the pleasant memories of Aunt Edna brought the stream to closure. Why? Because that's how you choose to remember her. She will stay in your mind forever in a positive place you created, a closure for Aunt Edna's life. She's gone, but it's all good. Closure opens new possibilities and sets you on a new course in life.

The Opposite of Closure: Being Stuck

Another way of understanding closure is by considering its opposite. At first glance, the opposite of "closed" might seem to be "open." In fact, the opposite of closure is what psychologists call "stuck." Stuck is a state where nothing positive seems to be happening, a state of frustration—maybe even torment.

If you are in this state now, notice how your thoughts and emotions repeat over and over again. The same themes keep coming up in your life, and you keep thinking about them in exactly the same way. This produces what psychologists call a "vicious circle." In reality, the purpose of this book is to help you escape being stuck by bringing issues that continue to plague you to closure.

Understanding Trauma

Now that we understand closure, let's apply it to trauma. What is trauma? According to Google, it is "a lasting emotional response to an event or series of events that are experienced as harmful or life-threatening." But let's just think of the most upsetting thing that has ever happened to you, something that you find hard to process, that preoccupies your thoughts, that interrupts your day, that causes you bad dreams, that you want to avoid and push out of your mind. Think of that dark place inside you where you dare not go. That's a definition of trauma that everyone can understand.

So, it makes sense to use trauma as the testing ground for any technique that claims to be as widely beneficial as guided imagery.

Of course, it is not only trauma that challenges your well-being and interferes with your happiness. Every psychological symptom, from anxiety and insomnia to depression and avoidance, has, at its core, something unfinished or incomplete. For any psychological issue to be resolved, it must, by definition, be completed. What I want to teach you is the ability to bring closure to all of the experiences in your life.

For now, please understand that trauma is only the most conspicuous and obvious example. Other examples include:

- Grief and loss
- Unforgiveness
- Perfectionism
- Self-criticism
- Self-sabotage
- Pessimism and depression
- Obsessive thoughts/compulsive behaviors
- Procrastination
- Anxiety and phobias

So, even if trauma isn't your personal issue, keep reading. This chapter lays the foundation for understanding the treatment of every other issue in the book.

.

But returning to trauma, you experience some statistically rare event that evokes an intense emotional reaction. The event may be so intense, in fact, that its basic sensory aspects—what you were seeing, hearing, touching, smelling, and tasting—become seared into the memory circuits of your brain. When these memories are triggered later on, they return with their full sensory intensity intact, which psychologists call "flashbacks."[2] Why is the impact of trauma/remembering traumatic events so powerful?

Guided Imagery vs. Cognitive Therapies: Engaging the Emotional Brain

The distinction between traditional cognitive therapies and guided imagery in treating trauma and emotional issues is rooted in how they engage different levels of brain processing. Cognitive therapies primarily work with the neocortex, focusing on logical reasoning and conscious thought, while guided imagery can access deeper structures like the limbic system, particularly the amygdala, which is central to emotional processing. Where cognitive approaches rely heavily on verbal communication and conscious analysis, guided imagery utilizes sensory experiences and visualization, more directly engaging the neural pathways associated with emotional memories. This allows guided imagery to tap into subconscious processes, potentially

---

2   Brewin, C. R. (2015). Re-experiencing traumatic events in PTSD: New avenues in research on intrusive memories and flashbacks. *European Journal of Psychotraumatology*, 6(1). doi.org/10.3402/ejpt.v6.27180

modifying more deeply-held emotional patterns, whereas cognitive therapies work mainly with conscious thoughts and beliefs.

While cognitive therapies can help patients understand their trauma rationally, this understanding doesn't always translate to emotional resolution. Guided imagery, on the other hand, aims to create new emotional experiences that can directly impact how traumatic memories are stored and experienced. Cognitive approaches may sometimes be hindered by conscious defense mechanisms, but guided imagery can potentially bypass these defenses by engaging the mind in a more receptive state. Furthermore, guided imagery offers a more holistic engagement, involving the whole person—mind, body, and emotions—potentially leading to more comprehensive healing, compared to cognitive therapies' primary focus on mental processes.

In terms of memory processing, while cognitive therapies can help reframe memories, they may not always change how these memories are fundamentally stored. Guided imagery, by creating vivid new experiences, may facilitate memory reconsolidation at a deeper neurological level. It also addresses somatic aspects of trauma that cognitive approaches might overlook. The immediacy of experience in guided imagery, creating present-tense scenarios that feel real to the brain, contrasts with cognitive therapies' focus on discussing past events. This allows for direct emotional experiences in a controlled setting, whereas in cognitive therapies, one can discuss emotions, but may not engage them as viscerally.

For instance, let's revisit Stafford's case. Had we relied solely on cognitive techniques, we might have fallen short of our therapeutic goals. Simply helping Stafford intellectually reframe the explosion and the soldiers' deaths would have been insufficient. Imagine suggesting that he merely think about the soldiers being carried off to heaven. For a battle-hardened veteran like Stafford, such an approach would likely feel patronizing and trivialize his profound experiences. Cognitive restructuring alone couldn't bridge the gap between his rational understanding and his deeply ingrained emotional responses. This is where guided imagery proved invaluable. It allowed Stafford to craft his own resolution, to experience it viscerally as if it were happening in real time. The power of this approach lies in its ability to engage both the emotional and rational parts of the brain simultaneously, creating a harmonious narrative that feels authentic and meaningful to the individual.

It's important to note that this comparison doesn't negate the value of cognitive therapies, which are evidence-based and effective for many individuals. Rather, it suggests that for some, particularly those dealing with deep-seated emotional trauma, integrating techniques like guided imagery that can access and modify emotional experiences more directly can be incredibly powerful. The ideal approach often involves a combination of both cognitive and experiential techniques, addressing both conscious thought patterns and deeper emotional processes for comprehensive treatment.

The Mind-Body Connection in Guided Imagery

To truly understand the power of guided imagery in treating trauma, we need to delve into the intricate relationship between the mind and body. This connection is at the heart of why guided imagery can be so effective in calming the nervous system and resolving traumatic experiences.

The Evolutionary Roots of Fear

Imagine two prehistoric humans emerging from their cave, scanning the savannah for potential threats. One sees a flash of orange in the distance and immediately retreats, crying, "Lion!" The other, more cavalier, dismisses it as merely flowers and ventures forth. Which of these early humans is more likely to survive and pass on their genes?

The answer lies in our evolutionary history. Those who were quick to perceive threats—even at the cost of frequent false alarms—were more likely to survive. This predisposition to fear in ambiguous situations kept our ancestors safe and allowed them to reproduce. As a result, we've inherited a brain that's finely tuned to detect and respond to potential dangers.

The Amygdala: Our Internal Alarm System

At the core of this threat detection system is the amygdala, an almond-shaped structure deep in the brain. The amygdala is our emotional sentinel, constantly scanning our environment for signs of danger. When it perceives a threat, it can trigger an immediate response—fight, flight, or freeze—before our conscious mind has even processed the information.

This rapid response system was crucial for survival in our evolutionary past. However, in cases of trauma, this same system can become overactive, leading to chronic anxiety and PTSD symptoms. The amygdala can become so sensitized that even harmless stimuli reminiscent of the original trauma can trigger a full-blown stress response.

Classical Conditioning and Trauma

The way the amygdala learns is through a process called classical conditioning. This was famously demonstrated in the (ethically questionable) "Little Albert" experiment,[3] where a child was conditioned to fear white, furry objects. This same process explains how trauma can generalize, causing a person to react fearfully to stimuli only tangentially related to their original traumatic experience.

Why Trauma Persists: The Role of Avoidance

Once a person has experienced trauma, they often learn to avoid situations that trigger their symptoms. While this provides short-term relief, it actually reinforces the fear response in the long term. The amygdala never gets the opportunity to learn that these situations are actually safe.

---

3   Watson, J. B. & Rayner, R. (1920). Conditioned emotional reactions. *Journal of Experimental Psychology*, 3(1), 1–14.

Guided Imagery: Rewiring the Nervous System

This is where guided imagery comes in. By providing a safe, controlled environment to confront and process traumatic memories, guided imagery allows for exposure without the risks associated with real-world situations. This exposure is crucial for the amygdala to "unlearn" its fear response.

But guided imagery goes a step further than mere exposure. It also provides an opportunity for closure—a way to bring the conscious mind (cortex) and the emotional brain (amygdala) into alignment. By creating vivid, emotionally resonant experiences of safety and resolution, guided imagery can help bridge the gap between our instinctual responses and our rational understanding.

In essence, guided imagery speaks the language of both the amygdala and the cortex. It provides the sensory-rich experiences that the amygdala understands, while also engaging the narrative and symbolic capacities of the conscious mind. This dual approach is what makes guided imagery so powerful in treating trauma and anxiety disorders.

As we move forward in this book, we'll explore specific techniques for using guided imagery to calm the nervous system, process traumatic memories, and create lasting change in both mind and body. By understanding this mind-body connection, we can harness the full potential of guided imagery as a healing tool.

Role of "Existential Assumptions" in Trauma

Traumatic events violate our most basic assumptions about what can and should happen in a human life. I call these "existential assumptions," or life assumptions, because they literally make everyday life possible. Most people believe that life is:

1. Mostly fair

2. Mostly safe

3. Mostly predictable

In addition, most of us would also agree that—on the whole—4) human beings are fundamentally good.

We learn these assumptions in early childhood, and they stick with us throughout our lives. When these assumptions are violated in a way that deeply affects our lives, we may work hard to figure out why. So, ask yourself this question: "Why do bad things happen to good people?"[4] Everyone wants to know, and no one has a completely satisfactory answer. What we can say is that fairness, safety, predictability, and human goodness form the psychological foundation that makes everything else possible in a human life. Jeopardize these assumptions, and you shake your psyche to its very foundations.

---

4   Kushner, H. S. (1981). *When Bad Things Happen to Good People.* Schocken Books.

So, this is the problem of trauma: trauma seems to prove the very opposite of the existential assumptions that lie at the foundations of everyday life. Trauma whispers to us, "You just thought life was fair, safe, and predictable—it's not. Human beings aren't fundamentally good—you were wrong. They're greedy and self-interested, and they'll exploit you any time they can get away with it." (Alas, research says that you are more likely to suffer PTSD symptoms when the traumatic event was caused or exacerbated by a human, rather than an act of nature.[5]) Try going through life without the existential assumptions as your working hypotheses—it's nearly impossible. How would you even get motivated in the morning if you believed life to be treacherous and human beings to be basically evil?

Immediately after trauma, people struggle to understand what happened. They want to sort out why the traumatic event occurred, how it might have been avoided, and who or what was responsible. Where was God when a tsunami killed hundreds of thousands? How exactly did a clergy person molest dozens of children? How could your trusted business partner abscond with tens of thousands of dollars when you'd known him since middle school?

In each such question, there is an effort to find some framework of meaning that would uncover essential information, bestow meaning on the event, defuse its emotional intensity, and bring closure. With the traumatic story completed, normal life, supported by the existential

---

5   World Health Organization. (2024, January 10). Post-traumatic stress disorder. who.int/news-room/fact-sheets/detail/post-traumatic-stress-disorder

assumptions mentioned above, can resume. Life makes sense again.

Until you place the trauma somewhere in your mind that makes it emotionally meaningful and complete (there's the concept of closure again), it will continue to insert itself into your conscious thoughts, interrupting a perfectly good spaghetti dinner or evening alone with *The Secret Lives of Mormon Wives* on Hulu. In the parlance of abnormal psychology, these are called "intrusive recollections," because they are as unwelcomed as an IRS audit.

As mentioned above, survivors of trauma may experience flashbacks, during which they see, hear, feel, smell, and taste the sensory experiences that accompanied the trauma, exactly as it occurred, as if the trauma was happening again. Sensory fragments of the traumatic experience can evoke the entire traumatic event.[6] A car backfires, and a war veteran hits the deck and rolls into a ditch. A rape victim is introduced to a man with a beard and immediately experiences revulsion—the rapist also sported a beard. Such intrusive recollections are always unwanted, tend to occur suddenly and unexpectedly, and may flood you with extreme anxiety. In a sense, this indicates that you are still in search of some framework of meaning whereby to assimilate the experience harmoniously into your life experience and beliefs. Again, the mind is like the stomach: whatever remains undigested may repeat on you.

---

6   Brewin, C. R. (2015). Re-experiencing traumatic events in PTSD: New avenues in research on intrusive memories and flashbacks. *European Journal of Psychotraumatology*, 6(1). doi.org/10.3402/ejpt.v6.27180

Self-Blame: An Incomplete Solution

Unfortunately, no one teaches you how to deal with trauma. You might be curious why this is, and the answer is unsettling. No one wants to admit that life can be unfair enough, unsafe enough, and unpredictable enough to shatter all of these existential assumptions. And no one wants to admit that there exists some evil side of human nature that allows some people to exploit others as if they were a harvest waiting to be reaped. Remember, inside all of us, there's a little child who demands and expects only happy endings.

As such, no one is ever psychologically prepared for trauma, and anyone who experiences trauma is necessarily forced into some kind of coping response. Most such coping responses are psychologically unhealthy, but it's best to view them as your best attempt to get back to a life that makes sense again, to restore your damaged existential foundations and go forward once again. Such solutions are best seen as a kind of compromise—something is gained and something is lost—as if you were saying "Yes, I have to carry the burden of the trauma with me, but at least it didn't destroy me." These are misguided attempts at recovery that at least allow you to resume some semblance of life, while insulating you from complete disaster.

So strong are you in your desire to have life make sense that you prefer to blame yourself rather than let life be random and destructive. Consider what psychologists call the "just world hypothesis."[7] The gist here is that, no matter

---

7   Pepper, S. C. (1942). *World Hypotheses: A Study in Evidence*. University of California Press.

what happens, you had it coming. Maybe you had it coming because you've been neglecting your child recently. Maybe because you bullied the red-haired kid in fourth grade, or returned to drinking without your husband's knowledge. Maybe you're just a bad person. Maybe you were the axe guy for Henry the VIII in another life. Regardless, disaster is your atonement. In that way, life still makes sense. In order to achieve closure, life has to make sense in some way to you.

Psychologist Dr. Martin Seligman introduced the term "explanatory style"—how we explain the world to ourselves. Here are some popular explanations:

- Life is not fair.
- Sometimes you are the windshield, sometimes you are the bug.
- All things work together for good to those who love God and are called according to his purpose. (Romans 5:28)
- Things always work out in the end, and if it's not worked out, it's not the end.
- What goes around comes around.
- God's ways are higher than your ways and God's thoughts are higher than your thoughts. (Isaiah 55:9)
- Karma can be a bitch.

Tony had severe symptoms of PTSD—all the usual suspects like intrusive recollections, powerful avoidance behaviors, and heightened arousal and anxiety. He was a miserable, trauma-plagued soul with serious insomnia. A major contributor to his unrest was guilt, a pervasive sense of feeling terribly guilty. You see, Tony was not only a veteran of the Gulf War, but also an inner-city police officer when he returned stateside. In the course of his tenure, Tony lost seven "brothers"—two soldiers and five policemen. Somehow, he survived, but was admittedly haunted by the deaths of his comrades on a nightly basis. How could he have saved them? There was no easy explanation for why these great guys died so young and so horribly.

Blame yourself, and you no longer have to admit that an anvil can fall out of the sky and randomly crush you and the people you love. The world at least follows some logic and becomes predictable again. As such, trauma naturally tends to produce guilt. Why did I (Tony) live while others died? Perhaps I am being punished for something. Perhaps I should punish myself.

Avoidance

Another way of coping with trauma is specifically addressed to the intense emotions and memories that accompany trauma: Go numb and deny it. Avoid reminders of it. Shut it all out. Repress it completely.

Lorinda was held up at gunpoint while working at a convenience store. Not only did she immediately quit her job, she began shopping only at large grocery stores. A war veteran refuses to watch war movies. A man molested by a priest refuses to drive within a mile of the church. This avoidance is not only behavioral, it is cognitive: You cope by putting it out of the mind. You actively suppress thoughts and emotions related to the traumatic event.

Numbness and avoidance are always functional, meaning that they help you stay afloat. First, they prevent you from reexperiencing the emotional intensity associated with the traumatic event. Second, your burial of the trauma serves to forestall consideration of the existential questions that trauma intrinsically creates—questions like "Why did this happen?" and "What is its meaning?" Avoiding such questions actually prevents you from making contact with some framework of meaning that might encapsulate, reinterpret, and defuse the intensity of the trauma.

You see, time does not heal emotional wounds. Feeling, expressing, releasing, and finding meaning heals wounds. Traumatic events are events in search of some framework or context that makes them meaningful. Such meaning provides the foundation for emotional release. The combination of letting go of the emotion and finding meaning for the trauma adds up to healing. Yes, it's letting go that is the great healer. But it is easier to let go of trauma when 1) there is a desire to let go, and 2) there is a place to release it. Go ahead and reread Stafford's and Todd's stories from Chapter One. Both were able to release their trauma by reinterpreting the traumatic event in ways that created hope.

Five Steps to Healing and Health

I described trauma specifically to bring prominent themes in psychopathology into focus. These themes were the role of existential assumptions in human life, the fact that every human being is on some kind of developmental path, and the need for emotional closure through a new framework of meaning.

Now I want to get more deeply into five steps that bring emotional closure and put you back on your personal developmental path. The first three of these steps are 1) remember, 2) feel, and 3) express. These three steps form a set strategically designed to prevent the emotional avoidance described above. Recall that emotional avoidance is a compromise solution. You at least get to stay somewhat on your personal developmental path. Yes, you may experience flashbacks. Yes, you may drive ten miles to avoid bridges. But at least you don't crash and burn, not entirely anyway. Remembering all the details of that trauma, feeling it inside, and expressing it to another person helps you to reclaim and consolidate a previously locked-away part of yourself and return it to the province of conscious awareness. We demolish your favorite coping mechanisms in order to rebuild new and better foundations. Psychologists refer to this as "exposure" (not the illegal kind). The treatment of trauma is basically stuck here, unless you proceed to the next two steps.

The last two steps are 4) release and 5) reframe. These two steps also form a set. The release, put simply, is to let go. Sometimes you just get tired of hurting and decide to let things go on your own. You refuse to allow your trauma to dominate your life. Most people, however, do not let go on their own. The reframe is intended to provide a new framework of meaning whereby the traumatic event is reinterpreted. This framework develops out of your own belief system—it's personalized to you. The release is then a natural consequence of this framework, because life now makes sense again.

In my last book, *Keep Pain in the Past*, I refer to this sequence of steps as "the Fritz" because of the contributions made by the not-famous-enough German psychotherapist Fritz Perls. Fritz belonged to a movement in psychology called Gestalt psychology, which emphasized that the mind seeks to interpret every experience as an integrated whole that requires closure. I'm in the habit of asking my patients and audiences, "How many of you mow 90 percent of your yard? Put away 75 percent of your dishes? Shave one leg?"

Let's look at the steps more deeply now, again with the idea that you'll be applying these to your situation, whatever it is, even if it's not trauma.

Step 1: Remember

The first step of the Fritz—remember—begins with your attempt to short-circuit avoidance by bringing all the details of the psychological issue to full awareness again. You need to recall as many details of your experience as possible, across all the senses. What were you seeing, hearing, touching, smelling, and tasting at the time when the traumatic event occurred? Beyond the sensory aspects, there's also the external and internal context of the event. What else was going on in the environment? What were you thinking when the event occurred? What aspects of the event stood out to you? What gave the event its unique or personal meaning for you? All the details of the event, no matter how trivial, need to surface. The trauma must be told. You must tell the tale in detail.

Step 2: Feel

Recalling the basic facts of the trauma sets up the second stage of the Fritz—feel. Feeling the emotions associated with the trauma is necessary because you are not just avoiding the facts, you are avoiding the emotional intensity of the trauma. It is the feelings you are hoping to never experience, because trauma, by definition, brings you face-to-face with feelings of intense fear, horror, defeat, devastation, hopelessness, etc. You are avoiding the memory specifically to avoid these feelings that accompany the trauma. As a hospital patient once told me about his service in the military, "I served in Vietnam and we don't talk about it." If he never talks about it, then he never has to feel the emotions associated with the trauma.

Stafford and Todd both expressed a sense of helplessness and injustice. You may have felt such emotions, but probably not while watching people burn alive or feeling your car run over them. This stage of the Fritz answers the question, "Why was the event traumatic for you? What meaning did the event have specifically for you?" Anger, fear, grief—all the emotions associated with the trauma—should surface here. If not, then it is unlikely that the treatment will be successful. Someone who reports the basic circumstances of the traumatic event with no feeling remains numb to the emotions of the event. No feeling equals no healing. Again, psychologists refer to this as exposure, and you can use exposure to defeat avoidance. But exposure is not enough; it is necessary, but not sufficient. Trauma must be felt to facilitate healing.

Step 3: Express

During the third step of the Fritz—express—you express all the emotions associated with the traumatic event. Expression is necessary for two reasons. First, feelings can remain completely internal—not shared with your therapist, and blocked from your own awareness. For this reason, it is not uncommon for completely unanticipated emotions to appear. The expression of grief, for example, may begin with sadness, but lead to anger. After the death of her husband, Jenny found herself not only sad, but also angry. She was angry because her husband had languished for several months in a nursing home, at great expense to their estate, which she and the children needed in order to survive financially. She was also angry because, at the young age of thirty-one, she was left alone, and she had never been alone before. Once Jenny became aware of her anger in therapy, she also felt guilty. Jenny felt guilty because her anger seemed selfish in the context of losing her husband. And because she could not easily stop the anger, she could also not stop the guilt.

Second, it is important to recognize that verbal expressions of feelings are not the feelings themselves, but instead merely representations of feelings—feelings put into words. As such, verbal expressions can be too abstract, symbolic, or intellectualized to have the power of actual experience. Again, trauma is not so much about the dry facts of the event as it is about the emotional impact of the event. The most emotionally powerful parts of the memory are often contained in the details and carried forward. One young lady told me, after being raped by an older man, "There was a cat in the room. Now I can't stand to be around cats." For this reason, every aspect of the memory must be shared, every last detail. You must empty your duffel bag completely. Of course, this can be done in the imagery, as you will see throughout this book.

As noted, the first three steps of the Fritz form a set. Remembering is cognitive, feeling is emotional, and expressing is behavioral. You may wish to think of them not so much as steps but as components—they can occur in any order, and may even be interdependent. For instance, subjects experiencing numbness listen to themselves trying to express their feelings, which in turn provokes more feelings. Once the floodgates open, awareness and expression constitute a powerful form of exposure that brings the total impact of the event into awareness. These first three steps, or components, provide the foundation for healing.

Step 4: Release

The fourth step of the Fritz—release—naturally follows the expression step. Sometimes the release happens automatically. You express your bottled-up emotions, feel better, and resolve to move forward on a new path. You "get it all out," as they say.

But the release does not always happen automatically. The expression of emotion lays the foundation for the release, but only you can decide to let go. Sometimes people want to hold onto their trauma for some reason. Example: Three people are in a car accident. One suffocates slowly under the weight of the car while begging for help. Both survivors develop trauma symptoms. One survivor keeps asking, "Why did this happen?" The other survivor becomes angry and resentful, and feels that the universe was grossly unfair by allowing the accident into their lives. Which person has a harder time finding emotional release? Anyone who makes demands on the universe—demands for fairness, demands for absolute safety, demands for a completely predictable world, demands that all humans be fundamentally good— nurtures a power connection to their trauma. Indeed, the opposite of release is holding on.

Why would you hold on to a trauma, the worst moment of your life? You wouldn't, unless there was a good reason to. And there is. Releasing the trauma means accepting the death of your friend—she's not coming back, and it's okay— or the boyfriend that doesn't love you anymore, that your bestie has a terminal illness and there's no cure, and so on. To release is to let go not only of the trauma, but also of the possibility of undoing it. The trauma did happen, and the release is to accept that it happened and make it okay. Thus, releasing and reframing go hand in hand. One can precede the other, or they can occur simultaneously. Releasing the horror puts a new frame on it, and putting a new frame on the horror facilitates release. Alas, the ticket to peace is acceptance.

Another reason to hold on to trauma is the perception that if you do let go of it, you are letting the perpetrator "get away with" their violation. Letting go of your pain and suffering can appear as if you are condoning bad behavior. But remember that releasing, letting go, forgiving—whatever you call it—never condones bad behavior; it only accepts that it happened and it's time to release it forever.

Step 5: Reframe

When release is not sufficient for recovery, the fifth stage of the Fritz—reframe—creates a new context for the trauma to be completed and come to closure. Life is unpredictable and often cruel. Live long enough, and you will experience some extreme event that begs for explanation. A police officer and his partner respond to a drug deal gone bad. A car chase ensues, followed by the collision of the police car and the drug dealer's SUV. One of the officers dies in the collision. How is this event constructed by the surviving officer? Perhaps he thinks, "My buddy lost his life in such a meaningless and tragic way" and goes on to develop trauma symptoms. Or, perhaps the partner thinks, "My buddy had a long record of distinguished service, and died honorably in pursuit of justice, the best death a person could hope for. Much better than having a heart attack or languishing in a nursing home." Thus reframed, the partner and his fellow officers feel affirmed by their comrade's heroic sacrifice. They view his courage as an example to be emulated. The difference between the two scenarios lies in the interpretation of the event. The mentally healthy framework lays the foundation for a sense of emotional release and closure.

Finding the right reframe is often key to emotional closure. I met a young woman who attended a Las Vegas concert where fifty-eight people were killed and another 422 wounded. She was told, by a well-meaning mental health professional, "Other people have had it worse." Such words, while intended to help, only hinder the healing process. They encourage the client to develop a sense of guilt about not being able to put their trauma behind them. Sure, other people had it worse—some were wounded, some actually died—but this young lady needs to remember the details of the shooting from her perspective, feel the raw emotions that accompanied the experience, and express these emotions in a safe environment. Next, the reframe is constructed to satisfy all of the powerful emotions inside you, moving you in the direction of closure. Healthy reframes for this young lady would include statements like, "I'm alive because I have some special purpose to perform" and "This experience has made me realize how valuable life is." Healthy actions would include raising public consciousness by speaking publicly about the experience and communicating with legislators. These ways of thinking and acting position the experience as a constructive force in her life and prevent her from becoming stuck.

Through the power of imagination, guided imagery provides a new context for traumatic experience that drastically changes its meaning. Occurring in the imagination, the reframed experience is as vivid and real as the original trauma, but the context of the experience is reframed, the experience completes itself in a new way. This could be, for example, an apology from a childhood abuser, a few moments on the other side with a loved one who has passed away, or simply words that empower the self, said to someone who has inflicted an injury. Back to Stafford and his reframe. Recall that the soldiers were taken away by angels in a really cool aircraft. This allowed him to accept their deaths and replace the tragedy with a sense of honor and closure about their lives. In other words, for Stafford to move on, he needed to experience the soldiers moving on. Note, however, that he first had to face the trauma and feel the horror of his helplessness, two of the first three stages of the Fritz.

No matter how good the reframe is, however, only you can decide to buy into the new interpretive framework as truth. Imagine that Stafford had demanded that his comrades not have died at all. Imagine that Todd had demanded that hitting the cyclist not have occurred. Such demands set up a scenario where time must be reversed in order for healing to occur. Obviously, that's not going to happen. For this reason, the reframe, no matter how good, requires something from you in order to be effective. In other words, the release is not something that passively happens to you. No matter how good the new interpretation might be, only you can accept the reframe as representing an important truth that puts you back on a new and healthier path. Always remember, time is not the healer you've been told it is. Letting go is active.

For this reason, it's important to understand going in that the purpose of treatment is acceptance—that is, letting go of the trauma, giving up whatever you might be holding on to. This leads to a point of decision: Do you continue with the trauma and sacrifice your life to it? Or, do you let go of the trauma and get back to being totally involved with the enjoyment of your life? Only you can actively choose to steer the ship in the direction of psychological health. A woman in therapy due to sexual abuse by her grandfather said, "I did not deserve to be touched that way. I was vulnerable because my family trusted him. I could certainly blame my parents, but I am going to move on, because I don't want to make his problem the centerpiece of my life." She recognized that the price of holding on to the trauma was eliminating the chance to live a happy and meaningful life.

Perhaps the best way to understand acceptance is to understand what acceptance is not. The opposite of letting go is holding on. The opposite of giving up is continued resistance, keeping up the fight, being stuck. Almost every human being has the experience of holding on to something to the bitter end. This suggests, then, that lack of acceptance is a kind of gritty stubbornness in the human spirit, a refusal of reality. Rather than work with reality as it is, we continue to insist that some imagined alternate reality be put in its place. The alternate reality is good, or at least not bad, whereas the "real reality," the one that actually occurred, is absolutely terrible. And all remains terrible, until we provide a new context and a new meaning.

How Does Guided Imagery Help?

Guided imagery integrates and improves upon all of the traditional forms of psychotherapy, simply because it allows you to experience alternative ways of thinking and a discovery of closure and peace, without leaving the safety of the therapy room. After all, guided imagery is as close to real experience as possible. In fact, because guided imagery has the ability to change the meaning of things and events, it provides supplementary experiences that you would never encounter on your own.

With guided imagery, Stafford and Todd were able to evaluate their traumatic events within a spiritual framework of meaning that they otherwise would never have experienced. Were these experiences authentic, or convenient fabrications designed to produce an effect? For Todd and Stafford, their experiences were completely consistent with their belief systems and thus, authentic to them, and therefore "transformative."

Case Study: Dale and Jill

Dale and Jill lost their son, not to death, but to schizophrenia. Jake, once a confident social butterfly, is now a recluse, sequestered in the back bedroom. For Dale and Jill, healing began with feeling the angst of their loss of the "old Jake" and acceptance that he would not be the physical therapist he previously aspired to be.

They were able to say goodbye to these dreams and accept his condition only when they realized that they still had a son who loved and needed them. Without that realization, their loss was the focus of their lives. With this realization, Dale and Jill could resolve to accept Jake's situation and not waste even more energy mired in suffering. Their goal was to help other parents with children diagnosed with mental illness.

First, however, they needed to remember, feel, and express— the first three stages of the Fritz. They had to acknowledge all of the dreams they had for Jake, and the dreams that he had for himself, and feel the emotions that would accompany the loss of these dreams. Only then could they release the negativity and commit themselves completely to a new path of acceptance and reframing their situation.

Case Study: Dylan

Dylan is a forty-something gay man who works as a legal professional. Dylan has spent most of his life grappling with his sexual orientation, only embracing an identity as a gay man within the last five years. Dylan had a few heterosexual romantic encounters and no committed relationships. So when he finally met Andrew, a guy he connected with, Dylan was smitten.

That's not necessarily a problem, but in this case, Andrew was engaged to be married to another man and on his way to Switzerland in a few weeks to live with his new husband. Andrew adored Dylan as well—the feelings were mutual. But Andrew did not want to break his existing relationship, and instead proceeded to marry and start a new life in Europe.

Unfortunately, Andrew found that he did not adjust well, and fell into loneliness, despair, and depression. One day, he reached out to Dylan for comfort and support, claiming that his marriage was empty and sometimes even abusive.

That was all that Dylan needed to hear. He reminded Andrew that he could come home, annul the marriage, and fall back into Dylan's loving arms forever and ever. Andrew never said no to the romantic fantasies offered up by Dylan. But he never said yes, either. Instead, Andrew seemed temporarily energized by Dylan's worship, only to sink back down again. Soon thereafter, the depression and loneliness worsening, Andrew took his life one day while his husband was at work.

Dylan was devastated by the news. He had lost not only his best friend and love interest, but also the person he was hitching his entire future on. In treatment, it became very important to examine the functional role that Dylan's fantasies about Andrew played in Dylan's life. With the fantasy of a partnership, Dylan didn't have to wade into the world of gay relationships. He didn't have to find friendships, activities, and causes. Instead, he could just hide in the fantasy that one day Andrew would return to the States and rescue Dylan from all of these challenges and responsibilities.

Was Andrew's death a trauma? It certainly was for Dylan, who was left wondering why he had ever met Andrew, and what meaning or message Andrew's death might have for his life. So, to say goodbye to Andrew was not only heart-wrenchingly sad, it was terrifying. A relationship with Andrew represented a happy life that Dylan could only imagine. Andrew's death felt like confirmation that Dylan would never be happy, never adjust to the gay world, never connect.

Instead of remaining stuck in these catastrophic fantasies, Dylan needed a way to reframe Andrew's passing as a personal or spiritual challenge that could redirect him in a healthier direction. Guided imagery helped Dylan say goodbye to Andrew, but there was much more work to be done. Dylan needed to face all that he had been avoiding by holding on to Andrew. Reframing meant that Dylan would need to admit to himself that he had been hiding in his Andrew fantasy—and then change it. Reframing meant facing his fears of starting again with no love interest, no romantic plan for the future. In fact, reframing Andrew's death meant putting a new interpretation on his entire social world. Releasing meant that Dylan would make peace with a life that no longer included regular contact with Andrew, and would instead choose to open himself to new possibilities of being gay and rewriting his life.

In the next chapter, we will explore the roots of guided imagery, probably not what you expect.

Chapter Three

A History of Guided Imagery

The history of guided imagery is as fascinating as it is ancient. In a recent paper, Max Highstein unraveled this rich tapestry, and I'd like to share some of his insights to set the stage for our exploration of this powerful technique.

Imagine, if you will, thirteenth-century Tibetan monks—several centuries before I was even a twinkle in my graduate school's eye—using meditation to envision Buddha curing diseases. But the roots of guided imagery stretch even further back, possibly to ancient Greece and Rome. Dr. Martin Rossman, co-founder of the Academy of Guided Imagery, tells us that the Greeks didn't just use imagery; they viewed imagination itself as an organ of the body.

This theme of imagery as a conduit to higher powers echoes across cultures. In shamanic traditions, practitioners journeyed through vivid mental landscapes to connect with spirit guides and ancestors, often accompanied by the hypnotic rhythms of drums and chanting. Meanwhile, in

China, healers used visualization to unblock the flow of *qi*, that vital life force believed to underpin both physical and mental health. (Picture, if you will, a kind of psychic Drano, clearing the blocked pipes of your inner plumbing.)

Fast-forward to 1985, and we find Jeanne Ackterberg penning *Imagery in Healing*, a book that became a cornerstone of alternative medicine. Ackterberg boldly claimed imagery as "the oldest and most powerful form of healing in the world," focusing on its ability to influence the course of illness and help patients manage pain and suffering.

The late 1980s saw Leslie Davenport founding a humanities program at Marion General Hospital and exploring the intersection of guided imagery with Tantric yoga. Her work delved into the Buddhist and Hindu practices of visualizing sacred images, based on the belief that deities could communicate directly through the mind's eye.

But it was Helen Bonny who truly pushed the envelope. In the 1970s, this intrepid music therapist combined imagery with music—and yes, even psychedelics—in her quest to expand consciousness for therapeutic purposes. The result? The Bonny Method of Guided Imagery and Music (GIM), a form of psychotherapy that's since been used to treat everything from physical ailments to addiction.

Despite these pioneers' efforts, mainstream medicine long regarded imagery as quackery. It took Carl and Stephanie Simonton's bestseller *Getting Well Again* to begin changing minds. They introduced the idea of a "cancer personality" and proposed that visualization and relaxation could aid in pain management and even survival.

Soon, imagery therapists were encouraging patients to visualize the destruction of cancer cells, sometimes in creative ways. Pac-Man gobbling up tumors, anyone? I used a similar approach myself, though I came to it independently, in a memorable session with a college student named Suzy (more on that later.)

Now, did these visualizations actually cure cancer? The research suggests not. But they did prove remarkably effective at alleviating the side effects of both the illness and its treatments. We're talking reduced nausea, fatigue, anxiety, and pain, along with improved quality of life and a bolstered will to fight. Highstein cites an impressive forty-six studies from the late '60s to the '90s demonstrating imagery's effectiveness in reducing anxiety, blood pressure, depression, and chemotherapy side effects.

As we entered the twenty-first century, research began to suggest that imagery might even influence immune activity at the cellular level. It's no wonder the American Cancer Society now endorses imagery as a valuable tool for cancer patients.

Yet, for all its proven benefits, guided imagery remains woefully underutilized in medicine and clinical psychology. Yes, it's found a place in spiritual practices, relaxation techniques, and coping strategies for severe illnesses. But I believe we've only scratched the surface of its potential, particularly in two critical areas: treating trauma and resolving grief.

In my research, I've discovered I'm not the first to recognize guided imagery's promise in these fields. But the literature is sparse, to say the least. It's this untapped potential that I aim to explore and expand upon in the pages that follow. So, buckle up, dear reader. We're about to embark on a journey through the mind's eye, one that promises to reveal new vistas in healing and personal growth.

Grief

While the literature on guided imagery for grief is sparse, it's not entirely barren. In 2012, clinical psychologist Dr. John Jordan wrote about incorporating imaginary conversations with the deceased in clinical settings. Though I haven't yet delved into his work, I find it fascinating that his approach mirrors my own technique of facilitating dialogues with departed loved ones to help my grieving patients find closure and peace.

Barbara Rubel, another voice in this field, emphasizes the power of these imaginary conversations. She sees them as catalysts for healing, allowing for catharsis (that Greek notion of emotional purging), the release of pent-up emotions, and the resolution of unfinished business with the deceased. It's a powerful cocktail of emotional processing.

However, Rubel cautions—and I wholeheartedly agree—that this isn't a DIY therapy. These guided journeys can stir up overwhelming emotions and unexpected responses. They're best navigated with a trained professional at the helm.

Trauma

When it comes to treating trauma and PTSD with guided imagery, we're still in the nursery, so to speak. The field is young, but it's growing rapidly. Recently, while poring over a chapter on guided imagery as a therapeutic tool for PTSD, I was struck by how much untapped potential still exists in this approach.

Take, for instance, the work of Straus, Calhoun, and Marx. These innovative clinicians developed a protocol for female survivors of sexual trauma that's both comprehensive and promising. Their method, aptly named Guided Imagery for Trauma (GIFT), is a twelve-week program that blends relaxation training, stress management, and self-efficacy skills. It's a multi-pronged approach, involving audio sessions, face-to-face therapy, and ongoing telephone support.

While GIFT shows great promise, it's a far cry from the one-session technique I've been refining over the past four decades. Different strokes for different folks, as they say.

Perhaps the closest cousin to my approach is a technique known as imaginal exposure. It's a type of exposure-based therapy designed to help people confront and overcome their traumas, along with the accompanying symptoms of fear, anxiety, intrusive memories, and avoidance behaviors. This method has its roots in the groundbreaking work of Dr.

Edna Foa, a University of Pennsylvania psychologist whose research on phobias, trauma, and OCD turned heads in the clinical world back in the 1980s.

The use of imagery to expose patients to their fears and phobias isn't new—it's been a staple in graduate psychology programs since the late '70s and early '80s. Techniques like systematic desensitization, imaginal exposure, and prolonged exposure have all aimed at helping patients master their traumas and phobias. Hypnotherapy, too, has played its part in this therapeutic orchestra.

My own brand of guided imagery? Well, it's a bit like Colonel Sanders's secret recipe—a unique blend of these various theories, techniques, and strategies, seasoned with my personal touch and four decades of clinical experience.

Sports and Performance

But let's step away from the therapist's couch for a moment and into the world of sports psychology. Here, guided imagery has found a home in the training regimens of athletes across all major sports (and yes, probably even pickleball). The goal? To train the brain to expect peak performance when it counts.

Think of it as mental weightlifting. By rehearsing successful outcomes in the mind's eye, athletes strengthen their neural pathways, making those ideal performances more likely in real life. It's not just about boosting performance, either—this mental rehearsal can also tame the butterflies of performance anxiety by increasing familiarity with high-pressure situations.

Don't just take my word for it, though. Household names like Conor McGregor and Michael Phelps swear by visualization techniques. Even Alex Honnold, that daredevil of free climbing, credits mental imagery as a crucial part of his preparation for scaling seemingly impossible rock faces.

And it's not just anecdotal evidence. Research has shown that mental practice can be almost as effective as physical practice in some cases. One study found that participants who only imagined exercising their little finger showed a 35 percent increase in finger strength. That's the mind-body connection in action, folks.

Guided Imagery and Me

My own journey with guided imagery began in graduate school, under the tutelage of Dr. Daniel Eckstein. His class on hypnosis and hypnotherapy opened my eyes to the power of the mind, and I eagerly held onto the two-page handout on hypnotic induction he provided. Little did I know then how those pages would shape my future practice.

It was during my time at the United States International University (now Alliant University) in San Diego that I had my first real taste of guided imagery's potential. A fellow student, Suzy, was struggling with severe gastrointestinal issues that had stumped her doctors. On a whim, and with the reckless enthusiasm of a graduate student not yet burdened by the weight of ethical considerations, I offered to hypnotize her.

Armed with nothing but my two-page handout and a vague recollection of the movie *Fantastic Voyage*, I guided Suzy on an internal journey to find the source of her pain. What transpired was nothing short of remarkable. Suzy described entering a cave with dark purple and violet walls, tearing off the colors like wallpaper, and discarding them in a waste basket.

Weeks later, Suzy reported that her symptoms—the daily vomiting, the blood in her urine, the abdominal cramps—had vanished following our session. It was a powerful lesson in the potential of the mind to influence the body.

Encouraged by this success, I conducted more sessions with Suzy, exploring the depths of suggestibility and the power of hypnosis. Word spread, and soon I found myself helping basketball players improve their game, assisting smokers in quitting, and aiding bodybuilders with their posing techniques. It was a heady time, full of discovery and possibility.

But, as with many things in life, the shine of novelty eventually wore off. People's reluctance to submit to hypnosis, stemming from fears of loss of control, coupled with research suggesting only a small percentage of the population was highly suggestible to hypnosis, led me to explore other avenues.

It wasn't until the 1990s, working with survivors of childhood sexual trauma, many diagnosed with dissociative identity disorder, that I truly began to understand the healing potential of guided imagery. These patients, with their ability to self-hypnotize and access traumatic memories, taught me the importance of facing trauma head-on: remember, feel, express, release, and then reframe. This five-step process, which I later dubbed "the Fritz" in honor of Fritz Perls, became my formula for healing (see Chapter Two).

What I learned was that it wasn't necessary to formally hypnotize people. A simple relaxation induction, far less intimidating to most patients, could open the door to that place of unfinished business that needed completion for true healing to occur. This realization has shaped my approach to guided imagery ever since, allowing me to help patients find closure and peace in ways I never imagined possible as a wide-eyed graduate student.

As we delve deeper into the applications of guided imagery in the chapters to come, remember this: what the mind can conceive, it can often achieve. Whether we're helping athletes visualize victory or guiding trauma survivors toward healing, the power of guided imagery lies in its ability to bridge the gap between imagination and reality, between the past and a hopeful future.

Gestalt Theory and the Evolution of My Approach

My journey into the world of guided imagery wouldn't be complete without mentioning the profound influence of

Gestalt psychology. During my academic years, I was introduced to Fritz Perls's brilliant theory on the importance of resolving "unfinished business" from our past. Perls's techniques, particularly the famous "empty chair" method— where one addresses an empty chair as if a significant figure from their past were sitting in it—opened my eyes to new possibilities in therapy.

Perls also advocated for letter writing as a means of closure. These weren't your everyday correspondence; they were powerful missives addressed to deceased loved ones, estranged partners, or anyone who had left this world before unresolved issues could be addressed. It was a way of speaking one's piece, even when the other party was no longer around to listen.

Somewhere along my academic journey, I was also exposed to guided imagery. Though the specific class eludes my memory, I recall learning about its applications in promoting relaxation and fostering positive mental states. Later, I discovered its use in enhancing athletic performance. But it was the synthesis of these various elements—relaxation induction, hypnosis, the concept of unfinished business, the need for closure, and guided imagery itself—that led me to develop the powerful therapeutic technique I use today.

I don't claim to have invented anything new. Guided imagery, after all, has roots that stretch back to antiquity. But I did find myself weaving together threads from various psychological tapestries. During my graduate training, I also encountered systematic desensitization and successive approximation— techniques that used closed-eye visualization of fear-inducing stimuli, combined with a state of relaxation, to help patients overcome their terrors.

It's worth noting that visualization is already a component of many mainstream psychological techniques. However, the specific application of guided imagery that I'll describe in the following chapters is, in my experience, quite rare. And that rarity is, frankly, distressing to me. I firmly believe this technique surpasses any existing treatment for grief and trauma, including the much-lauded EMDR (with all due respect to Ruth Shapiro). In fact, my four decades of clinical experience—encompassing over eighty thousand hours of psychotherapy—have shown me that the eye-movement component of EMDR isn't essential for successful outcomes.

What is crucial, as you'll discover throughout this book, is that the patient experiences the imagery as real. They need to say and hear what's necessary to let go, to complete, to release, to accept—whatever term best describes achieving closure, peace, and resolution of their suffering.

Why is this so vital? Because the mind's eye doesn't distinguish between imagination and reality—the nervous system processes both as real. Consider dreams, for instance. A dream is merely a movie of your own creation—you're the writer, director, and star. It's not actually happening. Yet how often have you woken up feeling terrified, amused, saddened, traumatized, angry, or joyous because of a dream's perceived reality?

One of my favorite anecdotes involves a couple in my office. The wife, clearly agitated, tells her husband, "In my dream last night, you were flirting with my best friend, Patricia, right in front of my face!"

The husband calmly responds, "That never happened."

To which she retorts, indignantly, "Right in front of my face!"

Her anger, insult, and offense at her husband's "shameful behavior" were palpable. The fact that it was "just a dream" was entirely irrelevant to her emotional experience.

This phenomenon extends to guided imagery as well. When people successfully complete a guided imagery session addressing trauma or achieving closure, they often refer to the visualized event as if it truly happened. The fact that it didn't occur in physical reality is immaterial—the emotional and psychological impacts are very real. They feel better, and that improvement endures. Closure is achieved.

In essence, guided imagery is a benevolent trick played on the nervous system. The individual engages with the fantasy so deeply that it becomes their reality.

Let me share one last example. A man came to me after a horrific head-on motorcycle accident that left him physically and emotionally paralyzed, unable to leave his couch or engage with life. After three months of conventional therapy, I finally persuaded him to participate in a guided imagery session to "finish" the traumatic scene—including the vivid detail of his stomach being pushed behind his right pectoral muscle.

Weeks after this session, he told me, "You know, Doc, I thought the whole thing was really hokey. But all I can tell you now is that I can get up off the couch and live again."

And isn't that, ultimately, what therapy is all about? Helping people get up off the couch—metaphorical or literal—and truly live again. As we delve deeper into the applications and techniques of guided imagery in the coming chapters, keep this transformative potential in mind. The power of the mind to heal itself, when properly guided, is truly remarkable.

Chapter Four

Treating Trauma with Guided Imagery

L ife, in all its complexity, can be both achingly beautiful and heart-wrenchingly cruel. This chapter, dear reader, may prove to be the most emotionally challenging yet ultimately uplifting journey you'll embark upon in this book. As M. Scott Peck so aptly put it on the first page of *The Road Less Traveled*, "Life is difficult." The Bible echoes this sentiment in Matthew 5:45, reminding us that God "makes his sun rise on the evil and on the good, and sends rain on the just and on the unjust." Or, to put it in more colloquial terms: shit happens.

When life's storms hit, they often leave in their wake a landscape of depression and anxiety. And when the tempest is particularly fierce, it can scar the psyche with trauma, trapping individuals in an endless loop of their worst experiences. The hallmarks of post-traumatic stress disorder (PTSD)—flashbacks, nightmares, intrusive memories, and a desperate avoidance of anything reminiscent of the trauma—become unwelcome companions on life's journey.

I won't sugarcoat it: if tales of profound human suffering make you squeamish, you might be tempted to skip this chapter. But I urge you to stay. For within these pages lie not just stories of unimaginable pain, but also testaments to the remarkable resilience of the human spirit. Each narrative I'm about to share is a beacon of hope, illuminating the transformative power of guided imagery in the face of trauma.

Amanda's Phoenix: Rising from the Ashes of Tragedy

Picture, if you will, the quintessential all-American girl next door. Long, sun-kissed hair framing a face that seems perpetually lit by a warm smile. That's Amanda. To know her is to be drawn into the orbit of her infectious joy. But beneath that radiant exterior lies a story of profound loss and incredible resilience.

Eight years ago, Amanda and her husband, Richard, lived through every parent's worst nightmare. A head-on collision on a busy highway tore their world apart, claiming the lives of both their children. Amanda's child from a previous relationship, also in the car, miraculously survived, though not unscathed. Richard, too, suffered significant injuries. But it was the unseen wounds—the emotional and psychological trauma—that threatened to consume them both.

Amanda emerged from the wreckage physically intact, but her soul bore the brunt of the impact. The tapestry of her psyche, once vibrant with hope and joy, now seemed irreparably torn. PTSD cast its long shadow over her life, manifesting in a constellation of symptoms: emotional numbness that left her feeling hollowed-out, a pervasive sense of meaninglessness that colored her world in shades of gray, and a gnawing survivor's guilt that whispered insidious questions. Why had she survived when her children hadn't? Wouldn't it have been better if she, too, had perished in the crash?

The accident rewired Amanda's nervous system, leaving her hypervigilant and easily startled. The simple act of being a passenger in a car—once so mundane—now felt like a herculean feat of courage. Driving near the crash site, or on similar highways, became an exercise in terror management. Her world contracted as she instinctively avoided any potential reminders of that fateful day.

But perhaps the most poignant symptom, the one that tugged at my heart as her psychologist, was the profound heaviness that seemed to weigh on Amanda's very being. It was as if the universe had cruelly fitted her with invisible ankle weights, forcing her to trudge through life while others walked unencumbered. The possibility of experiencing unbridled joy seemed as distant as the stars.

The accident hadn't just claimed lives; it had shaken the very foundations of Amanda and Richard's faith. Anger simmered beneath the surface, a palpable sense of betrayal by a god they once trusted implicitly. Church, once a sanctuary, became a battleground of conflicting emotions. The notion of God's love felt like a bitter joke, "Amazing Grace" a hollow platitude. Richard, unable to reconcile his loss with his faith, retreated from spirituality altogether. Amanda, desperate not to lose her connection to God along with everything else, went through the motions of belief, even as doubt gnawed at her core.

After more than a year of conventional therapy, I proposed a different approach. I invited Amanda and Richard to participate in a guided imagery session, hoping to offer them a path to closure and a means of reimagining their children in a place of peace. Amanda, her eyes reflecting a mix of trepidation and hope, agreed to take the journey.

What follows is Amanda's account of her guided imagery experience, in her own words.

> After going down the long staircase to the "movie theater" room, I sat down and I nervously waited to "start the movie." I finally pressed play, and I saw us all sitting at a large table at Buffalo Wild Wings. I wanted to stay there, in that moment, a little longer, because that's the last time we were all together, as a family, talking amongst ourselves. But I knew the purpose of this exercise was not for this, but I needed to fast-forward to the accident. I sped the movie up to right before leaving the restaurant. I went to the bathroom with Leila, as we had a little drive ahead of us before getting back to my mother-in-law's house. I remember reminding Leila (as I always would do) to not touch anything, because bathrooms are very dirty, and I remember even covering

the sensor that controls the automatic flush, because she hated it flushing before she was off the toilet! I remember rushing, because I wanted to say goodbye to my brother and sister-in-law, who met us for dinner (they had over an hour drive also).

It had been raining, nonstop, all day long. It was a light rain, but more than a mist. We ran out to the car, and got the kids in and belted, before getting into the front seats ourselves. The car ride was uneventful for the most part, as the kids fell asleep, and it got dark on the drive back. I fast-forwarded again until right when I saw two oncoming headlights turn into four, as a car headed into our lane. I remember looking at Rich, and seeing him try to jerk the steering wheel to the right as he said, "Oh shit!"

After that, it was quiet for a moment. Next, it was like I was trying to wake up and realize what was going on around me. I started hearing people say things about a possible fire. I tried looking around, and I could not see much, as it was still very dark and raining. I was in so much pain. My right wrist and left leg hurt so bad, and I didn't have a lot of space to turn around and see everybody. Ariana was verbal, and began asking what happened. I started asking if everyone was okay and then I said that it was going to be okay, and that we were in a car accident.

I do remember hearing Leila, our youngest daughter, crying and yelling at Ariana to get off of her. Ariana was very upset, saying, "Mommy, Leila is crying, telling me to get off of her, but I can't move!" I told Leila, "It's okay baby, people are coming, and they're gonna help." I couldn't see any of the kids, but I kept talking to them, in between my bouts of pain. Ariana then told me that she thought her legs were broken, because she couldn't feel or move them. I told her that this was possible, and I told her that my leg was broken too. I noticed a man, outside the car, with a bright light, walking around taking pictures (as evidenced by the sound the camera was making). I remember being so annoyed and upset, asking him, "Can you help?!" I never saw him again.

Ariana started crying and yelling, "Mommy, is Daddy okay? Is he dead?!" And I tried to watch for signs of breathing from Rich, as he was not conscious. His head hung down, with his hair in his face, and there were so many things blocking my view of him (deployed air bag, debris, etc.), but I did see his body/chest move very slightly with each breath. I told Ariana not to worry, that Daddy was alive and breathing, but he was asleep, because he got knocked out from the impact. I knew she was scared, as she started praying and saying sorry for all she had ever done wrong.

Everything was blurry, and people started taking my kids out of the car, taking them somewhere else. I could not see Ariana or Leila, but I heard a lady say, "She's vomiting," and I knew that she was with my Leila, because Leila would always vomit when she cried a lot. I looked to my right, and saw a man, sitting with my Maylee on the ground. I asked if she was okay, and although I don't remember what he said, I believed she was okay. I asked if he had a phone that I could use, and he ran over to let me use his. He told me to stay awake.

When the first responders finally arrived, I saw them take my Maylee on a stretcher, and I looked out the window, and saw her little arm hanging off the side of the stretcher, and it looked blue. This is when my fear kicked in. I told them to make sure she's breathing, because she looks blue! I stopped the movie here and started crying. This was the last time I'd see my Maylee, until I saw her in that tiny casket. This was so painful! Dr. Cortman asked if I felt stuck, and I said yes. When he asked me to share, I told him that I was worried that my little Leila, who had been vomiting, was in too much pain and was scared to be alone (because of her constant crying). But then I remembered that I would be able to talk to them again, and that I could imagine whatever I wanted to, in the moments that I was not focused on my girls.

Dr. Cortman offered the suggestion of angels comforting the girls, and I decided to rewind the movie to when I first noticed Maylee on the ground, with the man. I decided to imagine an angel coming down, cradling and embracing Maylee, before taking her by the hand, and walking toward her sister, Leila. I also imagined another angel coming down to Leila, and holding her, and telling her that everything is going to be okay, she's gonna be with her sister, and they can go when she's ready. I next imagined Maylee and Leila holding hands with each other and their angels, as they moved on to heaven. These angels did not have specific features, but were more like a warm light that engulfed and embraced the girls. I believe that the girls could see the angels' features, but I just knew that they were there.

This part of my experience made me feel a lot better, because I had been feeling so guilty that I could not get to them during their last moments before passing. I was angry with myself because I was *so* confident that they were going to be alright, and that I'd see them again. And if I knew that they would not survive, I would've died trying to get to them! Dr. Cortman then gave me an opportunity to speak to my girls again, and I was so excited to do so!

He told me to choose a meeting place of my choice, and I chose a playground. The girls always loved playgrounds! I met with Maylee, and I apologized for every time I had ever made her feel unhappy or upset, even for spanking her. I also apologized for the accident, and not being able to get to her in her last moments. She told me to not worry, she told me that she's okay, and no longer in pain. She said she misses us all, but knows that it won't be long until we're together again. She said she wants us all to find happiness, to be kind to and love one another, and she said that we'll understand more when we meet her in heaven. I told her that I love her so much, more than I could ever describe.

Next, I saw Leila and I rubbed her face with my face, like we used to do. I apologized to her, as well, and I told her that I wish I had known what was going to happen. She just looked at me, with a sad smile, and said that she and Maylee are not suffering. She said they are happy, and feel no pain. She said they are with God/Jesus, and they love it there. I hugged both Maylee and Leila, one in each arm, not wanting to let go, or let this moment end. But I knew that I could not stay here forever, and that Daddy wants to see them again too. I told them that Daddy would be saying hello as well, and they were glad.

Several feet away from the girls, I saw Jesus, waiting to reunite with them to return back to heaven. I approached Him, and fell to my knees, like the last time I saw him in a dream. He really didn't speak words, but I received his message, loud and clear. I need to love my husband and daughter; I need to help them learn what's most important in this life. I need to forgive myself for not being perfect, and to stop looking for faults everywhere. Sometimes things just happen. He said that bad things happen, but it doesn't lessen the love He has for us. We all have certain trials or tasks we must endure or complete, in order to learn what we need to learn, before we go Home to Him. I felt happy to send my Maylee and Leila off with Him, even though I wish they could stay here with us. I waved and said, "See you later!" before leaving the playground and coming back to our session in the living room of Dr. Cortman's home.

Doing this exercise helped me see the accident in a different light. Although it was still a traumatizing experience, I am able to not dwell on the little things that I had no control over. Being able to imagine angels with the girls before their passing helped me change my thoughts and fears of their last moments. Instead of fearing that their last moments were frightening, painful, or agonizing, I can now think of them as being peaceful, with them being greeted by angels and each other. This makes a huge difference in the amount of guilt that I have been carrying around with me.

> I still get some flashbacks, every once in a while, but I choose to imagine the angels, and how comforting they were, and it helps me deter the accompanying feelings of guilt that naturally arise with these memories/thoughts.

The Phoenix Rises: Amanda's Transformation

The guided imagery session proved to be a turning point in Amanda's healing journey. By allowing her to reframe her children's final moments, we unlocked a door to emotional release that had long been jammed shut.

The imagery of angels swooping in to rescue her children was more than just a comforting fantasy—it was a powerful psychological tool. It addressed the core of Amanda's guilt and helplessness, offering her a way to reconcile her inability to reach her children in those final moments with her deep-seated need to protect them.

Visualizing her children in the care of Jesus and his angels did more than just soothe Amanda's immediate pain. It allowed her to reimagine her children, not as victims frozen in a moment of terror, but as beings at peace, free from suffering, and imbued with a divine understanding of their fate. This new narrative gave Amanda permission to hope—hope for reunion, hope for understanding, hope for healing.

Of course, guided imagery isn't magic. It didn't bring Amanda's children back to life or erase the reality of her loss. What it did do, however, was offer her a new lens through which to view her tragedy. It gave her a tool to rewrite the story in her mind, not to deny what happened, but to find a way to live with it that didn't consume her entirely.

In the wake of the session, Amanda found herself able to breathe a little easier, to carry her grief with a touch more grace. The invisible ankle weights didn't disappear entirely, but they lightened, allowing her to take steps toward reclaiming joy in her life. It was a testament to the power of the mind to heal itself, when given the right tools and guidance.

Amanda's story serves as a powerful reminder that while we cannot always control the tragedies that befall us, we have more power than we realize to shape how we carry them. Through the alchemical process of guided imagery, Amanda transformed her pain into a bittersweet hope—a phoenix rising from the ashes of unimaginable loss.

While Amanda's story illustrates the power of guided imagery in healing recent trauma, one might wonder about the efficacy of this technique for wounds that have festered for decades. Can the passage of time calcify trauma, rendering it impervious to intervention? Or is it possible that even the most long-standing psychological injuries can be soothed by the balm of guided imagery? The remarkable story of Robert, a centenarian haunted by the ghosts of World War II, provides a compelling answer to these questions.

Robert's Story: Unshackling from the Chains of War

At the venerable age of 101, Robert cuts an impressive figure—a living bridge to a history that for most exists only in textbooks and fading photographs. But when he first crossed the threshold of my office, urged by his "child bride" wife of eighty-seven, Robert was a man at war with his own mind.

For eight decades, the specter of a flaming cockpit had stalked Robert's dreams, turning his nights into a relentless battlefield. His wife, Susan, driven to desperation by his nocturnal struggles—the thrashing, the moaning, the curses hurled at unseen enemies—had insisted he seek help. Little did they know that the true enemy lay not in the skies over Romania, but in a misinterpretation that had haunted Robert for eighty long years.

The nightmare that plagued Robert with clockwork regularity was always the same: "My plane was hit; a ball of fire blazed through the cockpit; I managed to escape, leaving George alone to perish on the floor."

It wasn't the inferno engulfing his aircraft that tormented Robert, nor the terrifying plummet from the sky. Instead, it was the crushing weight of guilt—the belief that he had abandoned his comrade, George, in a desperate bid for self-preservation.

This guilt had manifested in classic symptoms of post-traumatic stress disorder (PTSD), turning Robert's golden years into a crucible of unresolved anguish. It was as if time had stood still in that burning cockpit, with Robert forever poised on the knife-edge of that fateful decision.

Two sessions into our work together, I proposed we try guided imagery—a technique I hoped might finally allow Robert to digest the emotional shrapnel that had been lodged in his psyche since World War II. With the resilience that had carried him through a century of life, Robert agreed to this new mission.

After guiding Robert through a brief relaxation induction, I invited him to enter a movie theater of the mind. Here, we would revisit the trauma one last time, not as passive victims of memory, but as active observers seeking resolution.

As Robert settled into this imaginary cinema, the familiar scene began to unfold—his plane struck by enemy fire, flames licking at the cockpit. But this time, something was different. Robert's keen eyes, sharpened perhaps by decades of reflection, noticed a detail that had eluded him for eighty years: George's left arm lay limp in a way that spoke volumes. In that moment of clarity, Robert realized a profound truth— George was already dead when he made his escape.

The implications of this realization were staggering. For eight decades, Robert had been living in a silent horror movie of his own making, casting himself as the villain who abandoned his friend in the direst moment of need. But this narrative, which had colored his life for so long, was built on a misunderstanding. In reality, Robert had quickly assessed the situation, recognized that George was beyond help, and made the difficult but necessary decision to save himself.

This single moment of insight, facilitated by the safe space of guided imagery, accomplished what eighty years of waking life could not. It rewrote the narrative of that fateful day, transforming Robert from a self-perceived deserter to a clear-headed soldier who made the only choice he could under impossible circumstances.

The impact of this session was immediate and profound. According to both Robert and Susan, the nightmares that had haunted his sleep for so long vanished. The exploding plane, once a nightly visitor, retreated into the annals of memory where it belonged. At last, Robert had finished processing this traumatic experience.

The Takeaway: Time Is No Barrier to Healing

Robert's story serves as a powerful testament to the efficacy of guided imagery, even in cases where trauma has lingered for the better part of a century. It underscores several crucial points:

1. **The persistence of trauma:** Unresolved traumatic experiences can continue to affect individuals decades after the event, demonstrating the need for effective interventions regardless of when the trauma occurred.

2. **The power of perception:** Often, it's not the event itself but our interpretation of it that causes lasting psychological distress. Guided imagery can help

individuals reexamine these interpretations from a new perspective.

3. **The mind's capacity for healing:** Even after eighty years, Robert's mind was able to integrate new information and change his emotional response to the traumatic memory. This suggests that the human psyche retains its plasticity and capacity for healing well into advanced age.

4. **The importance of safe exploration:** Guided imagery provided Robert with a secure environment to revisit his trauma without being retraumatized, allowing for new insights to emerge.

5. **The potential for rapid change:** Despite the longevity of Robert's symptoms, a single moment of realization facilitated by guided imagery was enough to dramatically alter his experience. This highlights the potential for significant and swift change when the right conditions are met.

Robert's journey from a haunted centenarian to a man at peace with his past is a powerful reminder that it's never too late to address unresolved trauma. His story encourages us to view guided imagery not just as a therapeutic technique, but as a key that can unlock doors long thought rusted shut by the passage of time.

Beth's Odyssey: Navigating the Labyrinth of Trauma

In the tapestry of human experience, some threads are darker than others. Beth's story is woven with such threads, a testament to the complex interplay between trauma, addiction, and the remarkable resilience of the human spirit. Her journey taught me a crucial lesson: the folly of demanding sobriety as a prerequisite for therapy. For souls like Beth, healing the wounds of the past was the key that ultimately unlocked the door to sobriety.

Beth first came to me presenting symptoms of depression, but as we began to unravel the knot of her psyche, a more complex picture emerged. Like a palimpsest, layers of trauma were revealed, each one etched more deeply than the last. The first to surface was a summer of horror from when she was just six years old—a time when her maternal grandfather, tasked with her care, became her abuser.

As we continued our work, more painful episodes came to light: the cruel taunts of middle school bullies, the shattering betrayal of an abandoned engagement, the bitter taste of professional deceit. But it was the story of a night when Beth was twenty-one that would prove to be a linchpin in her healing journey.

Picture a warm Saturday evening, the air thick with possibility. Twenty-one-year-old Beth, all youthful exuberance and naive trust, agrees to go for a ride with a man she's just met. Part of her thrills at the adventure, while a small, insistent voice whispers caution. But the siren call of youthful invincibility drowns out that whisper, and Beth finds herself in the passenger seat of a stranger's car.

The night unfolds with the hazy rapidity of youth—a twelve-pack of Coors Light, attempts at worldly conversation, and then, like a switch being flipped, "Danny" makes his move. Beth, uncomfortable but not yet alarmed, goes along with a kiss. But when Danny's hands begin to roam, crossing boundaries she's not prepared to surrender, Beth pushes him away, her voice firm but still tinged with politeness, saying, "I'm not ready to do anything like this with you."

In that moment, something in Danny's eyes changes. The mask of civility slips, revealing a predator beneath. With a speed that leaves Beth reeling, he overpowers her, his hand clamping over her mouth to stifle her screams. The old Chevy's front seat becomes a battleground; the sound of a zipper being roughly pulled down a harbinger of the violation to come.

Beth's mind, faced with a horror too great to process, does what it learned to do all those summers ago with her grandfather. It disconnects, fleeing the scene of the crime even as her body remains. Dissociation, that double-edged sword of survival, allows her to retreat from "the ugliness of the deed," as she would later describe it.

In the aftermath, Danny's threats hang in the air like poison gas. He knows who she is, where she works. Any whisper against him would bring swift retribution. And so, Beth does what too many survivors do—she buries the story deep within herself, filing it away in some dusty, forgotten corner of her psyche.

For thirty-five years, that corner remained undisturbed. It wasn't until we began the delicate process of "defrosting" the memories of her grandfather's abuse that this long-buried trauma began to stir. The human mind, in its infinite complexity, often guards its secrets until it deems the time right for their unveiling.

I'll never forget the day Beth walked into my office, unaware of the emotional tsunami about to break. As she began to speak, it was as if time had collapsed. The twenty-one-year-old Beth and the woman before me merged, the story pouring out with a visceral immediacy that belied the decades that had passed. Tears flowed unceasingly, each one a testament to pain long suppressed.

In that raw, vulnerable moment, Beth demonstrated a truth I've observed in many survivors of childhood trauma: the ability of the mind to preserve memories in amber, keeping them vivid and immediate until they can be safely processed.

Despite the catharsis of unveiling this long-hidden trauma, Beth still felt unfinished. Her own investigative work had revealed that Danny was currently incarcerated for—in a twist of karmic justice—sexual assault and rape. Yet the knowledge of his punishment did little to quell the anger that still roiled within her.

It was then that I proposed a guided imagery session. I invited Beth to confront Danny in the safety of her mind's eye, protected by the barrier of prison plexiglass. As she sank into the comfort of my La-Z-Boy, eyes closed, responding with subtle finger movements, I guided her into a scene familiar from countless movies and TV shows.

In this imaginary space, Danny appeared as an older version of himself—thirty-five years had passed, after all. But I was careful to present him as diminished, weak, no longer the threat he once was. Beth, fully engaged in the imagery, began her confrontation.

Though the conversation happened in the silence of her mind, the intensity of Beth's emotions was palpable. Years of pent-up rage and pain poured forth as she castigated the man who had so callously violated her trust and her body.

When Beth had said her piece, I offered to speak as Danny, attempting to craft a response that would be therapeutic for Beth:

> I guess I deserve all of your rage and insults because I know I am guilty of hurting you and I don't even remember how many others. To be honest, it wasn't about sex, it was about feeling as if I had some control over something in my life. I always felt weak and inadequate and not very lovable. I didn't know how to talk to women and I never imagined that they could be interested in me. The only thing that made any sense was to overpower them to feel a sense of control or victory. I know that doesn't make anything better, but it wasn't about you or anything you did...

Before I could continue, Beth's eyes flew open, fixing me with a gaze of such intensity that it's seared into my memory. "I want him to apologize to me!" she demanded.

Without missing a beat, I shifted back into Danny's voice:

> I am so sorry for what I did to you. You didn't deserve any of it, it was all of my ugliness that I allowed to spill over onto your life and the lives of several others. For whatever it's worth, Beth, I am deeply ashamed of my behavior and how I hurt you. It's actually a relief to me that I will spend so many years behind bars, as I know that as long as I'm here, I won't hurt anybody again. Before I leave, please do whatever you need to do to feel better about yourself. And again, I'm very sorry.

The Alchemy of Healing: Beth's Transformation

In that moment, something profound shifted for Beth. The guided imagery session had given her what she needed most—not just the chance to express her long-suppressed rage, but to hear the apology she had been unconsciously craving for decades. It was a poignant reminder that in the realm of psychological healing, sometimes the most powerful moments come not from what we say, but from what we need to hear.

From that day forward, the rape lost its chokehold on Beth's psyche. It became a chapter in her life story, no longer defining her present or dictating her future. As we continued our work together, Beth courageously faced and processed other painful episodes from her past. Each confrontation, each resolution, was another step on her path to wholeness.

But perhaps the most remarkable transformation came when Beth, having cleared away the emotional debris of her past, was finally ready to confront her alcohol addiction. The bottle, long her refuge from unprocessed pain, lost its allure as she developed healthier coping mechanisms.

Today, seven years sober, Beth stands as a testament to the power of confronting our demons. She's no longer haunted by the ghosts of her past, having made peace with them through the alchemical process of guided imagery and therapeutic work.

Beth's journey underscores a crucial truth in trauma therapy: Sometimes, the path to sobriety and mental health isn't linear. For some, like Beth, we must first wade through the swamps of past trauma before we can climb the mountain of addiction recovery. It's a powerful reminder that healing, in all its forms, is a deeply personal journey—one that demands our respect, patience, and unwavering support as mental health professionals.

Sara's Symphony: Orchestrating Healing from Devastating Violence

Years ago, I had the privilege of co-authoring a book for Career Press about drug-free approaches to managing anxiety. My esteemed colleagues, Dr. Harold Shinitzky and Dr. Laurie-Ann O'Connor, and I penned *Take Control of Your Anxiety: A Drug-Free Approach to Living a Happy, Healthy Life*. Within its pages, we explored various facets of anxiety disorders, including the often-debilitating effects of post-traumatic stress disorder (PTSD).

It was in this chapter that I first shared Sara's story, a narrative so powerful it deserves retelling here. With Sara's permission, I'll recount her journey in her own words, a testament to the resilience of the human spirit and the transformative power of guided imagery.

Sara "Overcoming Trauma and PTSD"

When I was in my mid-twenties, I met a man that I eventually dated for about a year. Because of some circumstances, he opted to move five states away, and we lost contact with one another. Then, in my late thirties, I decided to look him up on Facebook, sent him a message, and we picked up our relationship where it had left off a decade earlier. Our newly reestablished friendship soon turned serious, and we begin to talk about a future together, and the option of my relocating closer to where he was living. We were both very excited about this new adventure in our lives, and what the future had in store for us. I trusted him like no other man I had ever been with, so much so that I gave him a key to my house so he could come and go as he pleased. I shared with him my every thought from daydreams to my deepest fears. I loved how comfortable it felt to be with him. We were so connected; I knew my life would never be the same. Little did I know how true that would be.

Another piece of the puzzle in my challenge was that this man was a master manipulator. As I was becoming reacquainted with him, I asked him if it would be okay to converse with some of his friends in the area in which he was living in, in an effort to get to know another side of this "old friend stranger" whom I hadn't seen or spoken to in many years. He was more than agreeable to this; he provided me with email addresses to two of his closest friends, with whom I began to converse. One of his friends had a girlfriend with whom I also conversed. I developed a good friendship with each of these three people via the internet, by way of email and instant messaging. But I later learned that this sociopath fabricated all these people for me to converse with, and they were all fake identities. *He* was actually portraying all three of these people. He used these three other "people" to further learn ways to control, manipulate, and attack me.

One winter night, just a few months after I had relocated my life to be closer to him, I woke to a knife-wielding, masked man at my bedside. He stabbed me fourteen times at various points on my body. I pleaded with him to leave. "Please, sir. Please go. Please leave," I begged over and over again. But he would not leave. In fact, he remained in my house for two hours, attempting to strangle me with a bed sheet, torturing me, and holding me hostage. He zip-tied my ankles and wrists and forced me to lay face-down in the hallway, bleeding, naked, and left to die. Just before he left, he told me that I was not to move for two hours, and that he would be waiting outside the door. If he saw any movement, he would come back in. I was terrified!

After some time had passed, I found the courage to scoop myself to a nearby bathroom. I found some nail clippers and was able to cut the zip-ties on my ankles, but I couldn't maneuver the clippers enough to reach the ties on my wrists, due to the severe slashes sustained from blocking my face from the knife. I made my way to the kitchen and found scissors, walked back to my seat, placed the scissors between my knees, and was able to use my knees to get the scissors to cut the zip-ties off my wrists. I allowed more time to pass, since I had no idea where he left for or if he would return. It was now about four hours after the attack and the sun was about to rise. I knew I needed to call 911, but he had stolen my cell phone. Cautiously, and with great fear, I went to the house next door and had them call for help. Police and rescue showed up, and I was airlifted to a trauma hospital, where my severe wounds could be tended to.

My parents were contacted in a meeting and flew out to me. After the necessary surgeries, I was discharged to the care of my parents. Three days after the attack, I returned to my house (the crime scene) to pack a few things to take with me, as I would be staying with my parents while I recuperated. I was adamant about finding a therapist to begin to help me overcome this horrific experience, and to begin to heal. Within a few weeks, I would also have to decide if I would be moving back to my new residence. My initial challenges and fears were numerous, largely because my attacker had not yet been arrested. With the help of the detectives on the case, I was able to determine the identity of the attacker: of all people, it was the one man I trusted more than anything...the man I had become reacquainted with!

I found myself looking over my shoulder a lot, wondering if he was around somewhere. I would go out only for a couple of hours for a doctor's appointment or a therapy session, and was always accompanied by someone. I would want to come back to the safety of my parents' home immediately, no errands, no stopping for lunch. A family member even went as far as to cover every window on the lower level of my house, so that I would be confident no one could see inside. I was terrified of the dark and would sleep minimally. I wasn't afraid of falling asleep, but of opening my eyes to someone at the bedside once again. I wouldn't even sleep in a bedroom alone. I felt that I needed constant protection to keep me safe. Within a couple weeks of the attack, I received great news. The man had been found, arrested, and taken to jail with no bond. Immediately, a new sense of freedom came over me. That would be the beginning of my return to normalcy. All the window coverings were removed that night, which was the first since the attack that I slept in a bedroom alone.

I remember one day being so emotionally overwhelmed that I laid on my bed for hours in the fetal position and sobbed, wondering if this was what my life was going to be like. Why me? What did I do to deserve such a thing? How dare he take my freedom and independence away! I found myself journaling on many occasions, especially on those sleepless nights. I was able to openly express many feelings of anger, hurt, resentment, sadness, and disbelief, and, eventually, some level of acceptance of the situation. Journaling was one of the most therapeutic interventions to assist in my emotional healing.

The weeks that followed brought challenges as well as successes. I had a lot of uncertainty about staying up north to live versus moving back to my short-lived new home. I made the decision to return to the place I had recently begun to call my home just a few months prior to live and make a fresh start. I was determined to not let that one person ruin my dream and continue to control all of my thoughts and actions. Now it was time to be in control again—control of my own thoughts, actions, and life choices. Three months after the attack, I moved back to live on my own. I was terrified. I kept nearly every light on at my house all night long. Bit by bit, my confidence grew, and I found myself forgetting to leave all the lights on and the quest for normalcy began. My main goal was to take back control of my life.

Once I returned to my new house, I researched to find a therapist who specialized in PTSD. I knew I still had a lot of healing to do both physically and emotionally. I had many new fears that had to be faced so that I could regain my life and independence. I feared the dark, I feared living alone, I feared being attacked again. My overall trust for people was minimal. I wouldn't leave home after sunset. I wouldn't walk anywhere where someone couldn't see me. I wouldn't use a sharp knife, let alone purchase a new set (my old set was collected as evidence). I had irrational thoughts of someone being in my house and hiding in a place as small as a cupboard. I feared masks of any sort. My heart would pound with anxiety and fear whenever I would encounter any one of those fears.

With the help of my therapist, Dr. Cortman, I was able to successfully overcome many of the fears that had come about as a result of the attack. My therapist worked with me, using many different options to work through my fears. The use of self-talk was one such option. When something scared me, I learned to tell myself I was safe, and that no one was going to hurt me. The night of the attack, the moon was full. I found myself being scared in subsequent months when the moon was full. My therapist helped me change my thought process from fearing the full moon to realizing the light of the moon helped me to make it to my neighbors safely to call for help. My therapist stated, "The full moon is our friend. It lights our path." Years after the attack, I still say that.

One pivotal session was when he had me do an exercise in imagery. He asked me to close my eyes and relax. Once relaxed, he asked me to envision the attacker (as I knew him in the relationship) sitting there. I described how I would approach my attacker, and tell him how I was feeling now, how I felt during the attack, and how angry I was at how, even after the attack, I still spent time and energy being fearful of so many things, and the impact his lies and deceit had on my current relationship. Toward the end of the session, I was able to say goodbye to him, and let him know how worthless he is, and that I would no longer allow him to take up my thoughts and my future stewing about what had happened. While I wasn't symptom-free, that session made a huge difference in my progress toward overcoming that tragic event. I would gradually find myself staying out after dark and leaving fewer lights on at home. In addition, I became less neurotic about looking in every room in my house upon returning from any place I had gone out to.

Part of my recovery was found in educating others on the dangers of the internet and social networking sites. Attending and speaking at victims' rights events was also very therapeutic, in the sense that it helped me find yet another positive in what some may consider to be a tragic event. One thing that my therapist told me was, "The worst day of your life can also be the best day of your life." Because of such opportunities to share and help others, I believe, wholeheartedly, that the night of my attack was one such instance.

Despite all the lies, deceit, and manipulation that I was subject to throughout the duration of my relationship with my attacker, I have once again learned to trust others and have even found love again. The occurrences of PTSD triggers are minimal, and I continue to challenge myself with lingering fears in an effort to fully recover.

Today, I continue to seek out opportunities to help keep others safe and to share my story in the hope that it will give others the strength to overcome whatever life's challenges may bring.

The Symphony of Healing: Sara's Transformation

Sara's journey from victim to survivor is a powerful illustration of the complex interplay between trauma, resilience, and therapeutic intervention. Her experience highlights several key aspects of trauma recovery and the efficacy of guided imagery:

1. **The pervasive nature of trauma:** Sara's story demonstrates how a single violent event can ripple through every aspect of a person's life, affecting their sense of safety, their relationships, and their very identity.

2. **The importance of professional support:** Sara's decision to seek therapy immediately after the attack likely played a crucial role in her recovery. It provided her with a safe space to process her trauma and learn coping strategies.

3. **The power of confronting fear:** Through therapy, Sara was able to face her fears head-on, gradually reclaiming the parts of her life that trauma had stolen from her.

4. **The transformative potential of guided imagery:** The pivotal moment in Sara's recovery came during a guided imagery session. This technique allowed her to confront her attacker in a safe, controlled environment, expressing her anger and pain without risk of further harm.

5. **The role of reframing:** By reimagining the full moon as a source of safety rather than fear, Sara was able to transform a trigger into a tool for healing.

6. **The healing power of helping others:** Sara found additional healing in sharing her story and educating others about internet safety, turning her traumatic experience into a force for positive change.

Sara's story serves as a beacon of hope, illustrating that even in the aftermath of unimaginable violence, healing is possible. Her journey reminds us that recovery is not about erasing the past, but about integrating it into our life story in a way that allows for growth, resilience, and even wisdom.

Lorenzo's Battlefield: Confronting the Echoes of War

While Sara's story speaks to the trauma of personal violence, Lorenzo's narrative opens a window into a different kind of psychological battlefield—the lingering effects of war. His tale is one that resonates with countless veterans, a reminder of the invisible scars that often accompany those who've served in combat zones.

Lorenzo, a Vietnam veteran, initially sought my help for family-related issues, particularly struggles with his adult daughter. Our sessions touched on various aspects of his life—his marriage, anger management techniques—but nothing that immediately signaled the presence of trauma or PTSD. Yet, as is often the case in therapy, the most profound revelations can emerge unexpectedly, like a long-buried landmine suddenly unearthed.

It was during one of our sessions that Lorenzo, with a mix of hesitation and determination, broached a subject he'd long kept buried. "May I talk to you about something unrelated to my family?" he asked, his usually confident voice tinged with uncertainty. "In fact, I don't like to talk about this with anyone."

As Lorenzo began to share, the weight of his unspoken burden became palpable. He spoke of his two tours in Vietnam with the Marines, acknowledging his relatively good fortune in returning home not just alive, but seemingly less scarred than many of his brothers-in-arms. "I don't spend a lot of my time thinking about terrible things that happened over there," he assured me, perhaps as much for his own benefit as mine. "But there is something..."

Lorenzo's story unfolded like a tightly wound spring finally released. He recounted a day that had etched itself into his memory with indelible ink—a day of camaraderie shattered by the sudden, violent intrusion of war's reality. "We were hit with a number of bombs, one right after another. Big explosions. Loud, really loud!"

The visceral nature of Lorenzo's description transported us both to that moment—the chaos, the fear, the instinctive dive for cover. "I know I stayed down for at least twenty minutes or so," he recalled, the uncertainty of those moments still evident in his voice decades later.

But it wasn't just the bombs that haunted Lorenzo. It was the loss—sudden, irreversible, and never fully processed. "We lost a guy in that bombing. You know, it's like it was yesterday in some ways. I liked that guy. I just remember that he was Jimmy."

The stark simplicity of that statement—"he was Jimmy"—encapsulated the personal nature of war's toll. Not just a soldier, not just a casualty, but Jimmy—a friend, a comrade, a life cut short.

Lorenzo's struggle wasn't with constant flashbacks or pervasive anxiety. His demon was more specific, more insidious. "The explosions are still with me," he confessed. "What's it been, forty-five years? I don't have a lot of nightmares or flashbacks like some of the guys at the VA. I don't go there anymore; I went a few times and I didn't like hearing the stories. But these bombs, it's like they come for me in the middle of the night in a deep sleep."

He described nights shattered by the phantom sounds of explosions, his body instinctively reacting as if he were back in the combat zone. "I'm just lying there quietly, deep in my sleep, and then boom!!! And I can feel myself dropping to the ground and anticipating more. Several booms, one after another, and I wake up in a cold sweat."

These nocturnal battles left Lorenzo exhausted and on edge, unable to return to sleep, forced to face the long, lonely hours until dawn. "I'm not even gonna try going back to sleep on those nights because I'm just so rattled, you know?"

Lorenzo's plea for help was heartfelt and urgent. Despite the medication he was taking for depression and sleep, the bombs in his mind continued their relentless assault. It was clear that a different approach was needed—one that could address the root of his trauma, rather than just managing its symptoms.

This is where the power of guided imagery came into play. I invited Lorenzo to revisit that day in Vietnam, not as a helpless participant, but as an observer with the power to change the narrative. In our session, we created a safe space—a movie theater in Lorenzo's mind—where he could watch the events unfold one last time.

The goal was multifaceted: to allow Lorenzo to process the trauma he had long suppressed, to say goodbye to Jimmy, and to help his younger self understand that he had survived, that he was safe, and that the war was truly over.

As Lorenzo engaged with the imagery, a profound shift occurred. He was able to speak to his younger self, to offer the reassurance and perspective that only time and distance could provide. He shook hands with that young Marine, promising him a future beyond the chaos and loss of that moment.

The results were nothing short of remarkable. Following our session, Lorenzo reported a cessation of his bombing-related nightmares and flashbacks. The war that had continued to rage in his subconscious for decades finally found its armistice.

"It finally feels over," Lorenzo shared in a subsequent session, his relief palpable. "And I am very relieved and thankful. It's such a relief to be done with that fucking war."

When I asked about Jimmy, Lorenzo's response was equally powerful. "Funny you should ask. I said goodbye to him during that imagery thing and I'm okay with him now. I haven't thought about him since that day."

Lorenzo's experience underscores the long-lasting impact of combat trauma and the potential of guided imagery to provide resolution even decades after the initial event. It demonstrates that it's never too late to address unresolved trauma, to say goodbye to the ghosts of the past, and to reclaim one's peace of mind.

His story is a powerful reminder of the invisible battles many veterans continue to fight long after they've left the combat zone. It highlights the importance of providing effective, targeted interventions that can help them finally lay down their psychological arms and find the peace they so richly deserve.

As mental health professionals, Lorenzo's journey challenges us to look beyond surface-level symptoms and to be open to addressing long-buried traumas that may be affecting our clients' well-being. It reminds us of the power of imagination and narrative in healing, and the profound impact we can have when we help our clients rewrite their stories of trauma into tales of resilience and recovery.

The Girl in the Road: Transforming Trauma's Indelible Image

In the tapestry of human suffering that I've encountered over my thirty-nine years of full-time private practice, certain threads stand out with stark clarity. Among these are the stories of sexual assault survivors and those who've lived through fatal car accidents. I've guided at least a dozen individuals through imagery exercises to help them process these profound traumas. But one story, in particular, illustrates the transformative power of guided imagery in healing even the most haunting of memories.

Trudy, a woman in her fifties, came to me bearing the weight of a tragedy she hadn't caused but couldn't shake. She had been the passenger in her sister's car when fate dealt a cruel hand, resulting in a head-on collision with another vehicle. But it wasn't the crash itself that tormented Trudy; it was its horrific aftermath.

In the chaotic moments following the impact, a young child—a girl of perhaps six or seven years—was catapulted through the windshield of the other car. This little stranger, whose name Trudy would never know, lay motionless on the pavement, a tragic tableau etched indelibly in Trudy's mind.

As Trudy recounted the scene, her pain was palpable, her curly blonde hair framing a face contorted with anguish. "I see that child lying face down in the road in her little pink onesie, motionless," she said, her words punctuated by sobs.

"It's a sick feeling in the pit of my stomach. Every time I see it, I feel so helpless and so horrified. I don't know what you could do about that, but this haunts me like a Hollywood horror movie. I can't seem to shake it."

The tragic irony of the situation wasn't lost on Trudy. She knew the child's mother had been driving under the influence and had failed to secure her daughter with a seatbelt. In a twist of fate that seemed to mock justice, the mother had survived while her innocent child perished.

Faced with Trudy's recurring nightmare, I knew we needed to employ guided imagery to reframe this traumatic memory. As always, we began with a journey to our metaphorical movie theater, where Trudy could safely revisit the accident from start to finish. But it was what came after that would prove transformative.

Knowing Trudy was a woman of deep faith, I saw an opportunity to leverage her beliefs in service of her healing. As the accident scene concluded, I guided Trudy to enter the movie herself, encouraging her to envision a transition to another realm—one where she could accompany the child beyond the tragedy of her earthly demise.

"Imagine, Trudy," I suggested, "that you're with this little girl in heaven, however you conceive it. See Jesus there, waiting to welcome her. Experience the joy and peace surrounding this child as she joins her loving Protector."

As Trudy immersed herself in this vision, I could see the tension in her face begin to soften. Building on this momentum, I invited her to participate in a celestial celebration.

"Now, Trudy, picture yourself joining hands with Jesus and the child. You're all dancing together in a joyous circle, like a heavenly version of 'Ring Around the Rosie,' but with lyrics of hope and redemption. Hear the music, feel the lightness and freedom of this moment."

As Trudy engaged with this imagery, a remarkable transformation occurred. The anguish that had clouded her features gave way to an expression of profound peace and joy. When she opened her eyes, they shimmered with tears, not of sorrow, but of cathartic release.

"It was one of the happiest moments of my life," Trudy shared, her voice filled with wonder. "And now, when I think of the child, I no longer see her on the road. I only see her dancing in heaven with Jesus. I can't conjure the bad image anymore, even if I try."

This profound shift in Trudy's perception illustrates the powerful alchemy of guided imagery. The horrific scene that had plagued her for so long—a memory her mind had repeatedly rejected as unacceptable and undigestible—was replaced by a vision of hope and eternal peace. It was as if her psyche, previously locked in an endless loop of entering an incorrect password, finally found the right key to process and integrate this traumatic experience.

By replacing the image of the lifeless child on the road with a vision of the same child celebrating in glory with Jesus, we created a new narrative that Trudy's mind could accept and, more importantly, find peace in.

The enduring nature of this transformation is perhaps the most compelling testament to the power of guided imagery. Five years after our session, Trudy's new vision remains vivid and comforting. "Oh yeah," she told me recently, her voice light, with a smile, "She's still in heaven and still dancing up a storm."

The Takeaway: The Transformative Power of Guided Imagery

Trudy's story encapsulates one of the most potent aspects of guided imagery in trauma therapy: its ability to replace stubborn, painful images with more hopeful and acceptable outcomes. This technique doesn't erase the reality of what happened, but it provides a new lens through which to view and integrate traumatic experiences.

As we conclude this journey through the landscape of trauma and healing, let Trudy's transformation serve as a beacon of hope. It reminds us that even the most haunting memories can be reframed, that the mind's eye can be redirected from scenes of horror to visions of peace. In the realm of guided imagery, we find not just a therapeutic technique, but a powerful tool for rewriting the narratives that shape our lives and our healing.

As we conclude our exploration of guided imagery in trauma treatment, we've witnessed its remarkable power to heal wounds both fresh and decades old. From Amanda's journey through the loss of her children to Robert's reconciliation with his wartime past, we've seen how this technique can reframe even the most deeply entrenched traumatic memories. Beth's confrontation with her assailant and Lorenzo's final farewell to the echoes of war further illustrate the versatility and potency of this approach.

These stories underscore a fundamental truth: trauma, at its core, is about unprocessed experience—moments frozen in time that the mind struggles to integrate. Guided imagery offers a unique key to unlock these frozen moments, allowing individuals to revisit, reframe, and ultimately release their traumatic burdens.

But the healing potential of guided imagery doesn't stop at the boundaries of trauma. As we turn the page to our next chapter, we'll discover how this same technique can be a powerful ally in navigating the turbulent waters of grief. While trauma and grief are distinct experiences, they often intertwine, each compounding the other's impact on the psyche.

Grief, like trauma, can leave us feeling stuck—trapped in a cycle of pain, longing, and unresolved emotions. It, too, represents a form of unfinished business, a struggle to come to terms with a reality our hearts resist accepting. As we'll see, the same principles that make guided imagery so effective in trauma treatment can be applied with equal power to the realm of loss and bereavement.

In the coming pages, we'll explore how guided imagery can help individuals say the goodbyes they never got to say, find closure in relationships cut short, and discover new ways of carrying their loved ones with them. We'll witness how this technique can transform the sharp pangs of recent loss and the dull ache of long-held grief alike.

As we transition from trauma to grief, keep in mind that the human mind's capacity for healing and growth remains our greatest ally. The stories you're about to encounter will demonstrate once again the remarkable resilience of the human spirit and the transformative power of imagination guided with purpose and compassion.

Let us now turn our attention to the delicate task of mending hearts broken by loss, armed with the knowledge that even in our darkest hours, the light of healing is within reach.

Chapter Five

Using Guided Imagery to Treat Grief-Stricken Patients

G rief, in its raw and unfiltered form, is a landscape of contradictions. It's a terrain where the familiar suddenly becomes alien, where time stretches and contracts in bewildering ways, and where the very foundations of our world seem to shift beneath our feet. If you've ever explored the literature on grief and the grieving process, you've likely encountered a barrage of well-intentioned but often vague advice: You'll have good days and bad. Sometimes your loved one will occupy your every thought; other times, you might go hours without thinking of them. Tears will come unbidden, then dry up just as suddenly. One day you'll feel you're turning a corner, only to find yourself plunged back into the depths the next.

Sound familiar? It should. These descriptions of grief are as common as they are frustratingly imprecise. But my intent here isn't to criticize these portrayals. Rather, I want to offer something more concrete, more hopeful—a beacon in the fog of loss.

What if I told you there was a way to find immediate relief, a path to peace about your loved one's passing, a method to rekindle hope for your future? I know, I know—I'm starting to sound like a late-night infomercial. But bear with me, because that's precisely what this chapter—indeed, this entire book—is about.

The treatment of grief, like most aspects of psychology and psychotherapy, is an evolving field. You're likely familiar with Elizabeth Kübler-Ross's groundbreaking work on the stages of grief, derived from her research with dying patients. Her model, proposing five stages—denial, anger, bargaining, depression, and acceptance—has become deeply ingrained in our cultural understanding of loss.

However, as influential as Kübler-Ross's work has been, it's crucial to recognize its limitations. Three common misconceptions have arisen from the widespread adoption of her model:

1. The assumption that research on dying patients can be universally applied to all who grieve.

2. The belief that these stages occur in a linear, non-overlapping sequence. (In reality, they're more akin to different facets of the grieving mindset, rather than predictable stages. Traveling north from Jacksonville, Florida, will invariably lead you into Georgia.

Expressing denial about your sister-in-law's death, however, won't necessarily usher in a stage of anger.)

3. The notion that grief resolves itself passively, through the mere passage of time. (As if depression magically transforms into acceptance without active engagement.)

As you'll discover in the pages that follow, successful resolution of grief hinges on *active* acceptance of the loss. This is where guided imagery comes into play. Rather than viewing grief as a passive, treacherous journey through uncharted emotional territory, what if you could take concrete steps to ease your pain and find peace? In the following five stories, you'll see that this isn't just wishful thinking—it's a powerful reality.

Ann's Story: Reclaiming Joy After Loss

Picture Ann: an eighty-four-year-old widow, a retired teacher from the Midwest with a heart of gold and a mind as sharp as a tack. Despite living alone—no children, no siblings, and as of a decade ago, no spouse—Ann radiates gratitude for her life. Her journey through loss and healing offers a poignant illustration of the transformative power of guided imagery.

Ann's story is one of two marriages: the first, a brief and tumultuous union with a man who, in retrospect, was grappling with mental illness. But it was her second marriage that defined her life. Raymond, about fifteen years Ann's senior, was, in her words, "a peach." (Do people still use that word?) Patient, wise, thoughtful, successful, and generous in both word and deed, Raymond was, to Ann, not just the best thing that ever happened to her—he was the top ten best things.

When asked where meeting Raymond ranked among the highlights of her life, Ann's response was unequivocal: "All ten."

Given the depth of their bond, watching Raymond succumb to the cruel grip of Alzheimer's disease was nothing short of devastating for Ann. As his primary caregiver, she found herself depleted—emotionally and physically. The vibrant, positive woman she'd always been seemed to fade, replaced by a version of herself plagued by anxiety and self-doubt. Even the most mundane daily tasks began to feel overwhelming.

The decision to move Raymond to a care facility was one of the hardest Ann had ever made. She would have continued caring for him at home indefinitely if not for the growing concern that he posed a danger to himself and potentially to her as his decision-making abilities and physical control deteriorated. The relief one might expect from relinquishing full-time caregiving responsibilities was overshadowed by crushing guilt. "What kind of wife would do such a thing to her loyal and devoted husband?" she agonized—a question that haunted her, feeding a cycle of self-doubt and shame.

In Raymond's final month, Ann found herself relying on Ativan, a mild tranquilizer prescribed for crisis situations. As her psychologist, I assured her that Raymond's passing would bring a kind of freedom to them both—his final days

The Guided Imagery Cure

were a shadow of his former self, and Ann was teetering on the edge of emotional collapse.

My goal was to guide Ann toward peace—to help her replace anxiety and self-torment with acceptance. I explained that the key to finding peace lay in accepting Raymond's imminent passing and his transition to the next realm which, in her belief system, meant heaven. I introduced the concept of guided imagery, explaining how it could provide her with one last meaningful exchange with Raymond before entrusting him to her conception of God.

Raymond passed away the following week, not unexpectedly. Ann's emotional state plummeted to depths I hadn't witnessed before—a potent cocktail of sadness, despondency, and dysphoria. Her grief wasn't rooted in the tragedy of his death (he was ninety-one, after all), nor in any sense of unfairness or shock. Rather, it stemmed from the overwhelming realization that the love of her life was gone, coupled with the nagging fear that she had somehow failed him in his final months by placing him in a facility. She felt adrift, lonely, ashamed—a ship without a rudder.

I grappled with the timing of the guided imagery exercise, wondering if it was too soon after Raymond's passing. However, I also recognized Ann's need for healing dialogue with Raymond—an opportunity to find peace with her choices, reaffirm their mutual love and devotion, and receive permission, in a sense, to continue with her life while knowing he was at peace.

Ann agreed to trust me with the guided imagery exercise just two sessions after Raymond's passing. While there's no prescribed timeline for introducing this procedure, it's a decision best made collaboratively between patient and therapist, with the patient feeling ready and capable of saying goodbye.

I began by guiding Ann through a progressive relaxation exercise, helping her calm her body one muscle group at a time. (I'll delve deeper into this process in Chapter Ten, "How to Do a Guided Imagery Session".) Ann, to her credit, moved into relaxation with remarkable ease. Comfortably settled in my La-Z-Boy chair, she responded to my questions with subtle finger movements, indicating that she was fully immersed in the experience, perceiving it as vividly as reality.

I facilitated a meeting between Ann and Raymond, ensuring she could see, hear, smell, and feel his presence until I was confident of a genuine connection. I encouraged them to embrace, allowing Ann to feel the warmth and safety of their marital bond. Then, drawing from the wealth of information Ann had shared about Raymond over our sessions, I began to speak on his behalf: "Ann, you've been a wonderful wife and partner to me. I'm deeply grateful for the two decades we shared—they were the happiest years of my life."

As I spoke, tears streamed steadily down Ann's cheeks. She dabbed at them with the tissues I'd provided, but they kept flowing—a testament to the depth of her emotions and the power of the experience.

Knowing what Ann needed to hear, I continued in Raymond's voice:

> I want you to know that I'm not in any pain. I'm well, truly at peace, and I have my full mental faculties again. My body is strong and able once more. While I can't reveal much about where I am, I can tell you that everything here is beautiful, and I'll be fine from now on. But Ann, I need you to understand that I won't be coming back to Earth to be with you. Still, I'll always care about you, and I need to know that you'll take care of yourself as much as you possibly can. Please, don't beat yourself up over putting me in the facility. It was exactly what needed to be done—honestly, given what a pain in the ass I was, you could've done it months earlier, and it would've been appropriate. Now, promise me that you'll take excellent care of yourself, just as you did for me.

In the silence of her mind, Ann made that vow to Raymond, treating it with the same gravity as her wedding vows. She responded to him, reaffirming what he already knew— that he was the love of her life, the very best thing that had ever happened to her. She pledged to honor his adult children, manage his financial legacy responsibly, and, most importantly, to take care of herself.

I ensured Ann had the opportunity to say everything she wanted and needed to say to Raymond. Even though they had the kind of marriage where positive words flowed freely, I wanted to make certain there would be nothing left unsaid, no regrets about words unspoken.

Using Guided Imagery to Treat Grief-Stricken Patients

When Ann raised her right index finger, signaling she had said and heard everything she needed, I guided them through one final, passionate embrace. Then, I asked Ann to watch as Raymond disappeared into the next realm.

The impact of the experience was immediately apparent. Ann reported feeling a profound sense of peace and acceptance regarding Raymond's death. Instead of isolating herself, she expressed a desire to go home and look at photos of their life together, finding joy in the memories, rather than sorrow.

In our next session, Ann described the guided imagery as a powerful experience. She emphasized how real it felt when Raymond told her he wouldn't be coming back—a painful truth, but one she needed to hear and accept. Notably, she found herself less fixated on memories of Raymond's declining days, instead recalling him as the younger, stronger, happier version of himself. We both agreed this was a positive shift in her grieving process.

Nine years later, I asked Ann to reflect on this experience, as if sharing it with the world. Here's what she wrote.

Ann's Guided Imagery Experience

I began seeing Dr. Cortman weekly in the fall of 2010, when my husband was showing signs of cognitive decline and I was experiencing a lot of anxiety. In the fall of 2011, my husband received a diagnosis of Alzheimer's disease. I was his caregiver for three and a half years until I had to place him in a memory care facility where he lived for four months, until he died in the fall of 2015.

I was heartbroken with sadness and loneliness and wondered if I would ever be okay again. I continued my weekly therapy, and a few weeks after my husband's death, Dr. Cortman said he would like to do a guided imagery exercise with me.

During this exercise, I remember the feelings were sadness and loss, and then Dr. Cortman took me to the happiness that Raymond (my husband) and I shared.

He talked about our love for each other and our joy-filled lives. I had seen Dr. Cortman for five years, so he had heard a lot about Raymond—the kind of person he was and how well he treated me.

It was an emotional experience for me. I remember exactly where I was sitting in the office and the feeling of tears rolling down my cheeks.

Near the end of the exercise, Dr. Cortman spoke to me as if he was Raymond, and I will never forget the words: "Ann, I am not coming back, and I want you to be happy."

Dr. Cortman gave me a minute, and then he closed the exercise. I felt so relaxed and peaceful.

The guided imagery was a meaningful and powerful experience, and my grieving seemed to be on a different footing after that.

This took place a number of years ago as I write this, but the details I have mentioned are etched in my memory in a very positive way.

The Takeaway

The most crucial aspect of this procedure was Ann's complete immersion in the process. From the outset, it was clear she was relaxed, and engaged with every instruction. The tears she shed were a powerful indicator that the experience was registering on an emotional level—always an excellent sign.

Raymond's statement that he "will not be coming back" provided Ann with the clarity she needed. It gave her permission, in a sense, to stop pining for his return and instead focus on honoring his memory through self-care and embracing life.

The guided imagery session made an immediate and profound difference in Ann's life. It gave her a new direction, infused with hope, peace, and acceptance—a perspective that has only solidified over the past decade.

Father Sean's Symphony of Grief and Healing

One of the most moving guided imagery experiences in my clinical career occurred about eight years ago with Father Sean, a semi-retired priest. Our initial work together focused on helping him navigate the challenges of workplace bullying within the church hierarchy. I was disheartened to learn that his efforts to address what appeared to be systemic abuse had fallen on deaf ears. Our task, then, was to help Father Sean find healthy ways to cope with this unresolved situation.

He made remarkable progress, completely reframing his perspective and embarking on a journey of self-empowered recovery. I was delighted with his transformation. However, just months after we concluded our active treatment, Father Sean returned with an even more daunting challenge: he had lost the love of his life—his biological mother.

A woman in her late eighties still living in Ireland, Sean's mother was, by his account, the proudest and most supportive mother imaginable. If you found yourself in line behind her at the grocery store, you'd invariably learn that her son was a priest living in America before you reached the checkout. While a mother's love and pride in her male offspring is well-documented in many cultures (Irish, Italian, Hispanic, Chinese, to name a few), Sean's relationship with his mother seemed to transcend even these norms. As a priest without a life partner, Sean had no one else to provide the unconditional support and love he received from his dear mother.

The rapport we had built during our previous work allowed me to suggest guided imagery with confidence. Father Sean embraced the idea immediately, eager to try the technique in our next session.

Sean dove headfirst into the procedure. He hadn't been present for his mother's passing, having thought he would have more time to return to Ireland for a final visit. While he made it back for the funeral, he felt the acute loss of not having had the chance to express all the things he had always felt, but struggled to articulate outside of the occasional birthday or Mother's Day card.

What made this experience particularly special for both of us was Sean's desire to express himself aloud rather than in the silence of his mind. He responded quickly to the relaxation component of the procedure and chose to meet his mother in a favorite park they had enjoyed during his childhood outside of Dublin. To his delight, he found himself easily transported back to the beauty of his homeland. He envisioned his mother as a younger version of herself, one who could climb hills and walk alongside him with ease.

Speaking as Sean's mother, I conveyed the pride and love she felt for her son:

> I am the proudest mother in the world because, with all the troubles in the church, my son is a true servant of God, a living disciple of our Lord, Christ Jesus. I will be able to proudly tell the Lord, "Look at my son, he is your good and faithful servant, always doing your work, like the Shepherd guiding his flock." My Lord is welcoming me home, dear son, so I shan't stay long. I will soon be reunited with your father. As you know, I have missed him greatly over the years. We both know that he struggled with drinking. But he loved you, Sean, and he loved your brothers, both of them. I

am seeking peace, and I'm relieved to leave behind my earthly body—you know how much I suffered in the last years of my life. I have no regrets when it comes to you. I have loved and adored you from the beginning, son, and I always will.

Sean's response was both passionate and heartbreaking. With eyes closed but brimming with tears, he exclaimed, "Oh Momma! I love you so! Momma, my dearest mother, I miss you every day!" He held his arms out, as if reaching for an embrace he had long yearned for. "Please Momma, don't go! I know, I know you must. But what am I to do? Where am I to go? How can I do this life without you?" His sobs were palpable, and I found myself silently weeping too, my thoughts drifting to my own mother, then suffering through the ravages of Alzheimer's disease.

In Sean's mind, his mother gently dried his tears and reassured him. "You will always be with me, son, as I will never be far away from you. You have honored me with your life. Now please, let me be at rest with our Lord, Sean. I will always love you!"

Sean spoke once more, his voice thick with emotion but tinged with acceptance. "It's okay, Momma. It's okay, you go. I will be okay. But I will always miss you!"

The guided imagery exercise marked the final session dedicated to processing Sean's loss of his mother. When I inquired about it later, he said simply, "I'm okay with Mom's passing now. It's in a good place. And she is with our Lord. I have you to thank."

The Takeaway

I've always taught my patients that the core of healing is to feel, express, and then release, making it possible to reframe whatever painful material we're dealing with. Father Sean grieved for his mother acutely during that session, anguishing over her loss and fearing life without her. But then he made a decision to release her and, simultaneously, committed to being well despite her absence for the rest of his life. It was indeed a way to reframe the loss of the president of his fan club.

This reframing didn't mean Sean would stop missing his mother. Rather, it allowed him to know he would be okay, and to hope that she would be happy in her new reality, with a whole new audience to regale with stories about her son, the priest.

Sean's story beautifully illustrates the power of guided imagery in providing a space for expressing deep-seated emotions, finding closure, and reframing loss in a way that allows for continued growth and healing.

Rachel's Story: Finding Peace Without Faith

A question that often arises during my public speaking engagements about guided imagery and connecting with the deceased is, "What if the patient is an atheist and doesn't believe in an afterlife?" Rachel's story provides a compelling answer to this query.

At eighty-two years old, Rachel was a force of nature—a Jewish-American atheist who stood barely 4'11" but filled every room with her larger-than-life personality. Kind, loving, and unapologetically opinionated on all subjects, Rachel was the type of person who inspired strong reactions. In her community, people either loved her or found her challenging. As for me, she made me laugh (and sometimes treated me to homemade brownies), so I counted myself firmly in the "love" camp.

Rachel had three children, but it was her daughter Sarah who was the light of her life. Sarah was the kind of child you might special-order from a catalog if such a thing were possible—brilliant, accomplished, funny, and personable. But Sarah's vibrant life was cut tragically short by an aggressive breast cancer before she even reached forty. Although Rachel had two surviving adult children, she would confide in me, "Between you, me, and that dying plant over there, Sarah was my favorite."

Given Rachel's deep love for her daughter, the idea of a guided imagery session was an easy sell. At the very least, it would provide her with an opportunity to envision her wonderful daughter one more time. However, Rachel's atheism presented a unique challenge. This wouldn't be a "Goodbye for now, I'll see you later in the next life" scenario, but rather a "Goodbye forever, because there is no next life" situation.

As we prepared for the guided imagery session, I explained the procedure and guided Rachel through the relaxation induction. Unlike some of my other patients, Rachel didn't need to imagine borrowing her daughter from a heavenly mansion—such concepts held no meaning in her belief system. Instead, they met at their favorite coffee shop, a place where Rachel had always felt comfortable meeting loved ones.

I ensured that Rachel could envision every detail of the coffee shop before having Sarah walk in and sit down. As Sarah took her seat across the table, I had her excitedly greet Rachel. "Hi, Mom!" I could already see tears forming in Rachel's eyes, a sign that she was fully engaged in the experience.

Taking the lead, I spoke as Sarah, drawing from the background Rachel had shared with me over our sessions: "I wanted to see you one more time, Mom, because I know how brokenhearted you've been since my passing. I mean, how could you not be, as wonderful as I am?" I saw a smile break through Rachel's tears, confirming that my attempt to capture Sarah's sense of humor had hit the mark.

I continued:

> But seriously, Mom, the connection I had with you, I'm sure you know, surpassed my connection with anyone else, including my husband. There's no one I would laugh with more often. No one I'd rather see a girly movie with and share a large popcorn and a package of Kleenex! And no one I'd rather try out a new recipe with, or even just chat about the events of the day.

Sure, you were and always will be my mother, but did I ever tell you, you were also my best friend? So I wanted to come back one more time, not just to remind you of how happy and successful my short life on Earth was, but also to tell you that you were the very best part of it.

I allowed a moment for these words to sink in as Rachel emptied my tissue box. Then, I gave her the opportunity to respond to her lovely daughter. While I couldn't hear Rachel's exact words, I had a good idea of what she might say based on our many conversations about Sarah. I told Rachel:

Make sure that you let her know the joy she brought into your life, the many things you learned from her, and what you will always carry forward from her. Please tell her that you are a better person because of her and the world is a better place because she was here. It's also okay, Rachel, to tell her not only that she was your favorite child, but that she was your very favorite human being. And if there is anything beyond this life, tell her, "You are the one I want to be roommates with, wherever they send us."

Rachel laughed out loud at this last line, recognizing it as the kind of banter she and Sarah might have enjoyed over a cup of coffee. She knew she needed to say goodbye to Sarah, but she also knew that she would proudly keep her daughter in her heart for the rest of her life.

In a cruel twist of fate, Rachel faced another loss just three months after our guided imagery session when her husband suffered a fatal heart attack. Once again, we found ourselves navigating the turbulent waters of grief.

The Takeaway

The key lesson from Rachel's experience, at least for me, is that one doesn't need to believe in an afterlife, a God, or a heaven to find peace after losing a loved one. Rachel never believed she would see either her daughter or her husband again, but she benefited immensely from the realization that she could find peace about their passing and keep the beautiful contributions they made to her life alive long after they were gone.

Rachel's story demonstrates that guided imagery can be a powerful tool for processing grief and finding closure, regardless of one's spiritual beliefs. It's not about imagining a reunion in an afterlife, but about creating a space to say the things left unsaid, to honor the relationship, and to find a way to carry the love and memories forward into the future.

For atheists or those without belief in an afterlife, guided imagery can still provide:

1. An opportunity to "speak" with the deceased and express unresolved feelings

2. A chance to revisit cherished memories and reinforce the positive impact the loved one had on their life

3. A framework for finding meaning in the relationship and the loss

4. A path to acceptance and peace, even in the absence of belief in continued existence

Rachel's experience reminds us that the power of guided imagery lies not in its ability to connect us with an afterlife, but in its capacity to help us process our grief, honor our relationships, and find a way to move forward while keeping the memory of our loved ones alive in our hearts.

Richard's Story: Navigating the Complexities of Spousal Loss

In the 1970s, researchers Holmes and Rahe developed what they called the "Social Readjustment Scale." You may have encountered it—a list of life events, each assigned a point value based on its potential stress impact. I vividly recall that receiving a speeding ticket was worth eleven points, as was simply going through the Christmas season. But at the top of their list, deemed the most stressful life event and scoring a full 100 points, was the loss of a spouse.[8]

According to their research, accumulating more than three hundred points in any twelve-month period predicted a 90 percent chance of hospitalization in the following year. This underscores just how profoundly the loss of a spouse can impact one's well-being. (As an aside, after many years of clinical practice, I would argue that the death of a child is at least as impactful as the death of a spouse, if not more so.)

---

8   Holmes, T. H., & Rahe, R. H. (1967). The Social Readjustment Rating Scale. *Journal of Psychosomatic Research*, 11(2), 213–218. doi.org/10.1016/0022-3999(67)90010-4

Given the intense stress associated with spousal loss, it's not surprising that at any given time, somewhere between 10 and 25 percent of my patients are widows or widowers, grappling with acute grief over the loss of a partner.

Richard's story exemplifies this struggle. He and his wife, Mary, had been together for half a century, forty-eight of those years in marriage. The bond forged over such an expanse of time is so profound that research consistently shows that, in at least half of such cases, the surviving spouse doesn't live more than six months after their partner's passing. This holds true even when there's no prior diagnosed illness in the surviving spouse. It's a stark reminder that losing a long-term partner ranks among the greatest known health risks.

Richard was living this reality, though his experience was nuanced in ways that challenged the idealized notion of spousal grief. He loved Mary, of that he had no doubt. But she was also, in his words, "a pain in the ass"—often controlling, pushy, and bossy. Richard admitted that he didn't always enjoy living with her. Yet he struggled to voice these truths, constrained by the unspoken societal code that dictates, "You don't speak ill of the dead."

In our sessions, Richard didn't exclusively extol Mary's virtues. He sometimes mentioned her shortcomings, particularly her failure to take proper care of herself. At the same time, he was uncomfortable criticizing her in front of others. Our task was to help Richard express his complex feelings and empower him to move forward in life without Mary.

There were aspects of his life with Mary that Richard certainly wouldn't miss. In her final years, as her health declined, he had become her caregiver—a role he likened to an impossible mission. He joked that caring for her should have been accompanied by the theme from *Mission: Impossible*.

You might wonder: does this ambivalence change the grieving process? The answer is both yes and no. Over the years, I've worked with a handful of patients who were puzzled by their lack of sadness following a spouse's death. Invariably, these were individuals whose marriages had been painful, sad, or even abusive. They questioned what was wrong with them for not missing their spouse, to which I would often respond, "You don't miss influenza when it passes."

But in most marriages, including Richard's, there's a mix of good and bad, things to miss and things to gladly leave behind. While Richard's marriage had its challenges, he knew that Mary loved him, even if she was difficult at times, and particularly so at the end of her life.

We decided to attempt a guided imagery session about a year and a half after Mary's passing. To be honest, Richard's engagement with the process was not as smooth as I typically hope for. He appeared fidgety, not fully relaxed, and opened his eyes a couple of times during the procedure. Nevertheless, we persevered.

I encouraged Richard to express his love for Mary, to share how much he missed her and how challenging widowerhood had been. I urged him to voice anything he felt was important to get off his chest. In turn, I had Mary convey her love for

Richard and her gratitude for his care, especially during her final days. Throughout the session, I noticed tears in Richard's eyes—a sign that, despite his apparent restlessness, the procedure was evoking strong emotions.

Interestingly, the benefits of the guided imagery didn't manifest immediately for Richard. It wasn't until a couple of weeks after our session that he began to notice a gradual shift in his feelings. He found himself feeling better and more at peace with Mary's passing, though the change was subtle and incremental rather than sudden.

In Richard's own words:

> My wife of forty-eight years suffered a stroke and died after a terrible six-month ordeal. We were very good friends and enjoyed our life together and each other's company. My wife's unexpected death left me in an awful place. I saw Dr. Cortman, a therapist, for over a year to help get my life together. This helped a little, but still left me with a huge, empty, painful hole. One day the doctor suggested using "guided imagery" to help me say goodbye to my wife and for me to accept what has happened. Along with the immense pain and emptiness, I had been feeling a sense of guilt from not helping her more. Of course, this wasn't true, but nonetheless present. I knew nothing about the guided imagery process and was skeptical, but decided to do it since I trusted my therapist. He seemed to know when it should be done. He was right on. It took a few visits, and eventually I felt the large load had been taken off of me. The process was extremely emotional and painful,

but gave me a good foundation to manage my life going forward. So here I am now, over two years after my loss, some better and still working to improve. A degree of hope has arisen.

The Takeaway

Richard's experience with guided imagery offers two crucial insights:

1. **Timing is everything:** Sometimes, people aren't ready to say goodbye, and forcing the procedure too soon almost guarantees a less successful outcome. I waited over a year with Richard, sensing he needed more time to process his loss before engaging in this intense emotional work.

2. **Delayed gratification:** Richard's story challenges the notion that the effects of guided imagery should be immediate and dramatic. He didn't experience an instant transformation; instead, he noticed a gradual lightening of his emotional burden over the weeks following our session. This reminds us that healing is often a subtle, incremental process, rather than a sudden breakthrough.

Richard's journey underscores the complexity of grief, especially in long-term relationships where love and frustration, joy and resentment often coexist. It demonstrates that guided imagery can be effective even when the immediate experience seems less than ideal, and that healing from loss is a unique and personal journey that doesn't always follow a predictable timeline.

Just when I thought I knew everything about this procedure, Richard's experience taught me new lessons about patience, timing, and the subtle ways in which healing can manifest. It's a powerful reminder of the need for flexibility and individualization in our approach to grief therapy.

Sherry's Story: Healing from the Unthinkable

As alluded to earlier, if there's anything as devastating as—or perhaps even more devastating than—the death of a long-term partner, it's the loss of a child. The death of a child at any age seems to fly in the face of life's perceived order, predictability, and fairness. As one of my patients poignantly stated on the very day of his son's death, "It shouldn't be like this... He should bury me, not the other way around."

Sherry's story exemplifies why psychologists like me show up for work day after day. With the warmest of smiles, a complete acceptance of responsibility for her life choices, and a sincere desire for change, Sherry was the kind of patient therapists dream of. Oh, for a caseload of Sherrys!

When we met, Sherry was in her early sixties. She and her husband had adopted two children from a Ukrainian orphanage—a toddler and an infant. Their decision to adopt was born from a desire to fill the void of childlessness by offering two children, who had little hope for a happy and healthy life, the golden opportunity that life in America promised.

But reality rarely aligns perfectly with our dreams. Years after coming to the States with her adoptive parents, Natasha, the older child, reported experiencing sexual abuse during her childhood. The details were never clear, but what was evident was that Natasha lived her life as if she were "damaged goods," grappling with drug and alcohol abuse, truancy, emotional instability, and relationships with "shady people" who were quick to take advantage of her vulnerability. Her tumultuous journey included bouts of homelessness, rape, and even a period of erotic dancing.

Tragically, Natasha's life was cut short in a motorcycle accident just before her twenty-first birthday. She was inebriated at the time of the crash, a final, fatal manifestation of her ongoing struggles.

Sherry was devastated. She had loved Natasha deeply, and despite all her efforts to create a happy life for her daughter, it had ended in tragedy, failure, and utter disappointment. As we had seen with Rachel's story, Natasha was Sherry's favorite person, the one she most delighted in whenever they were together. They shared inside jokes, a passion for music, dogs, and the Boston Red Sox—a relationship of reciprocal adoration.

Now, that vibrant connection was gone, and Sherry needed help to somehow digest this tragedy and hopefully make peace with Natasha's life. She had a plan: she wanted to read me journal entries from the last four years of her and Natasha's life together. An accomplished journal writer, Sherry was certain that going through this time together with an understanding therapist could lead her to a place where she might make sense of the premature ending of Natasha's life.

I shared my idea of eventually incorporating a guided imagery technique, hoping to promote some semblance of closure for Sherry. It took several years of therapy to digest the journal entries and the significance of the shared experiences of Sherry, Natasha, and the rest of the family. Through this process, Sherry began to realize that despite the challenges and suffering, Natasha's life contained many joyous moments and seemed, overall, to be a life with meaning and worth, despite its brevity.

A turning point came when I shared with Sherry the perspective that, "While we all die eventually, we don't have the same amount of time here to live." This seemed to resonate deeply with her.

Gradually, Sherry came to accept that, for whatever reason, Natasha's life on Earth was over. She chose to believe that there was another reality beyond this one, and Natasha had simply arrived there faster than the rest of the family. Even more importantly, Sherry began to see Natasha's passing as part of God's plan, a perspective that brought her a measure of peace.

Due to the hard work she invested in therapy, Sherry was making progress in coming to terms with Natasha's death. However, we both agreed that attempting the guided imagery exercise could provide another opportunity to connect with Natasha and to hear and say whatever remained unfinished from before her tragic death.

As I've mentioned before, Sherry was an ideal patient, and I knew she would easily comply with the relaxation component of the imagery. Her history with meditation made the process of visual imagery relatively easy for her. As she recounts in her story below, she took a moment to envision what Natasha would be wearing when they met again, starting with the ever-present Chuck Taylor sneakers. From there, Natasha's image came into clear focus, and the two were able to connect deeply.

As usual, I spoke on Natasha's behalf, drawing from the years of stories Sherry had shared with me in therapy. Here's Sherry's account of her experience:

> I have been working with Dr. Cortman for some time, since the unexpected death of my twenty-one-year-old daughter in a motorcycle accident. We've made a lot of progress in processing my emotions over Natasha's death, and Dr. C. had been suggesting guided imagery as a way to bring some more closure and allow me to move forward in life with less of a weight. But what with COVID-19 taking away in-person sessions, the ongoing issues and traumas associated with my son's alcoholism, and my general hesitancy, I had not taken him up on his suggestions.
>
> But finally, I was ready to try. So he picked a date. I was a little anxious and excited. I wondered what it would be like. But my anxiety revealed itself on my way to see Dr. Cortman, since twice I made wrong turns on a route that I knew well. Which meant I arrived nearly ten minutes late!

As he always does, Dr. C. put me at ease and laughed with me over my wrong turns. The room was quiet. I laid down on the sofa and closed my eyes. The sofa was comfortable, which helped. Dr. C. had me do some deep breathing. I liked starting that way. I do a lot of yoga and know how to use deep breathing to relax.

Next, Dr. C. guided me through an image of a blue glow, or light or energy, slowly replacing the red (hotter, more emotional) energy in my body. We began in my chest, envisioning the blue light, replacing the red light, moving slowly up through my head, and then down my back, arms, and the rest of my body to my toes. (I found this to be a very helpful visualization and have called on it a few times since when I can sense my anxiety and want to calm down.)

Then, through imagery, we went on a walk together, down some stairs, where my relaxed body became more relaxed and heavier with each step. Finally, we reached the final landing, maybe three flights down, where there was a corridor and doors along the corner. Dr. C. told me to stop in front of one of the doors and let me know that when I opened it, I would be in the space where Natasha would be able to meet me.

He suggested I think of a place that made me happy, or where I had good memories, or would like being with Natasha. He gave me some examples, all of which were good and fit my relationship with Natasha because they were places we had been together—the beach, a baseball game (that made me smile). But I wasn't sure where I was going to find myself, until I opened the door. And in the instant I opened the door, I knew where I was going—in the woods on a beautiful sunny day. I would meet Natasha under the trees, with the comfort of nature and fresh air all around us.

Then Dr. C. told me Natasha was there and I should start to see her. I slowly built up an image of her in my mind. Again, until that moment, I had no idea what she should be wearing. But then I knew. I started with her feet. She was wearing Chuck Taylors. Of course she was wearing Chuck Taylors when she came to see me, because she always wore Chuck Taylors. They are the low-cut version and black-and-white. Except Natasha's Chuck Taylors are faded black and very well worn. Just writing about them now brings a smile to my face. And once her shoes were there, the rest was easy—the tight, faded, skinny blue jeans, the gray Boston Bruins T-shirt with the big B logo across the front, and Natasha's hair down, long and wavy. Her face was harder to visualize, but her body was not, and I knew she was there. I knew she was there by the emotions I felt—I could feel the love in my heart for her and from her. My eyes teared, not from sorrow, but because it had been so long since I had been with her.

And then we had a conversation. Dr. C. spoke for Natasha. She let me know that she had permission for a short while to be with me, that she was glad to see me (and I was very glad to see her). She wanted me to know that she was okay, and that she was sorry for all the craziness that she put us through not keeping herself safe. And that she loved me and knew that one day we would be together again. And I let her know how much I loved her and missed her, and that I kept her in my heart always and that she was always with me.

And then she let me know she had to leave. And she gave me a long, deep hug. Which, as I write this, I realize that was what she did the last time I saw her alive. Her dad and I stopped by to see her on our way to the airport, and she gave me a hug like she was never going to see me again. I will never forget the way she felt.

And then she was gone. And Dr. C. brought me back to the present. And I was okay—still relaxed. I felt the emotional impact of our meeting, but I also felt good.

I was in great spirits on my way home. On the way, I followed my impulse to stop at Oscar Scherer State Park. It was right on the way, and I had always wanted to go there. The park was beautiful, and I found myself walking under a canopy, beautiful trees and palms. I knew I came there because she was bringing me to a place where I could continue to feel our meeting.

That was when I knew why I saw her in the woods. Not because she was going to bring me to Oscar Scherer, but because the two places we have chosen to memorialize her are in the woods. One is in Sarasota, where there is a beautiful hammock under a graceful oak, where the sitter can gaze at a mangrove bayou. The other is in Cambridge, where her ashes will be laid to rest next to a granite boulder on a wooded hillside. Both are places where I go to bring her to me, so of course that is why we met in the woods.

> The whole experience has helped me find peace—
> knowing that our love is secure and I can continue to
> bring her to me.

The Takeaway

Sherry's story underscores several crucial aspects of using guided imagery in grief therapy, particularly when dealing with the profound loss of a child:

1. **Timing is crucial:** It took several years of traditional therapy before Sherry was ready for the guided imagery session. This preparatory work allowed her to process her grief and come to terms with Natasha's life story, making the imagery experience more impactful.

2. **The power of sensory details:** Sherry's focus on Natasha's Chuck Taylor sneakers as a starting point demonstrates how powerful sensory details can be in making the imagery feel real and immediate.

3. **Flexibility in belief systems:** While Sherry had come to believe in an afterlife, the imagery didn't rely heavily on this concept. Instead, it focused on creating a space for meaningful communication and closure.

4. **The importance of unfinished business:** The imagery provided an opportunity for Sherry to express things left unsaid and to hear what she needed to hear from Natasha.

5. **Integration of the loss:** The experience helped Sherry find a way to keep Natasha's memory alive while also

accepting her passing, illustrating how guided imagery can aid in the healthy integration of loss into one's life narrative.

6. **Lasting impact:** Sherry's positive response to the imagery, both immediately and in the following days, showcases the potential of this technique to create enduring shifts in how one relates to their loss.

Sure, training in yoga, meditation, and visualization can be helpful for a guided imagery procedure. But not all patients will have this background. What Sherry's story truly highlights is that the most important component of a successful grief-related imagery experience is an attitude that declares, "I am ready to meet my person and say goodbye to them."

In fact, this readiness and openness is the single best predictor of success in all guided imagery exercises, regardless of the specific issue being addressed. Sherry's journey from devastating loss to a place of acceptance and peace serves as a powerful testament to the healing potential of guided imagery when coupled with thorough therapeutic preparation and a willing, open mindset.

As we conclude our exploration of guided imagery in grief therapy, we've witnessed its remarkable ability to facilitate healing across a spectrum of loss experiences. From Ann's journey through spousal bereavement to Sherry's heart-wrenching process of coming to terms with her daughter's untimely death, we've seen how this technique can offer solace, closure, and a path forward even in the face of life's most profound sorrows.

These stories underscore several key insights:

1. Guided imagery is adaptable to diverse belief systems, as demonstrated by Rachel's atheistic perspective and Father Sean's deep faith.

2. The technique can be effective even when the loss is complicated by ambivalent feelings, as in Richard's case.

3. Timing and readiness are crucial factors in the success of guided imagery interventions.

4. The power of this approach lies not in recreating reality, but in providing a safe space for emotional expression and resolution of unfinished business.

5. The benefits of guided imagery can be immediate or gradual, highlighting the need for patience and individualized approaches in grief therapy.

Perhaps most importantly, these narratives remind us that while grief is a universal human experience, each person's journey through loss is unique. Guided imagery offers a flexible, personalized tool that can be tailored to meet the specific needs of each grieving individual.

As we turn the page to our next chapter, we confront an even more complex, and often stigmatized, form of loss: death by suicide. The grief that follows suicide is often complicated by feelings of guilt, anger, and unanswered questions. It presents unique challenges that can make the healing process particularly difficult.

Yet, as we'll discover, the same principles that make guided imagery so effective in addressing other forms of grief can be powerfully applied to the aftermath of suicide. We'll explore how this technique can help survivors navigate the turbulent emotions, find answers to haunting questions, and eventually forge a path toward healing and understanding.

In the coming pages, we'll witness how guided imagery can provide a safe space for confronting the painful realities of suicide while also offering opportunities for resolution and peace. We'll see how it can help survivors have the conversations they never got to have, express the emotions they've been struggling to process, and find ways to honor their loved ones' memories while moving forward with their own lives.

As we transition from grief in general to the specific challenges of suicide bereavement, keep in mind that the human capacity for resilience and healing remains our greatest ally. The stories you're about to encounter will once again demonstrate the remarkable adaptability of the human spirit and the transformative power of imagination guided with purpose and compassion.

Let us now turn our attention to those grappling with the aftermath of suicide, armed with the knowledge that, even in the face of this most devastating loss, the light of healing is within reach.

Chapter Six

Healing in the Wake of Suicide

F ew life events carry the devastating impact of suicide on a family. Research consistently shows that survivors of suicide grapple with a complex tapestry of emotions: shock, devastation, hopelessness, guilt, rage, shame, and overwhelming feelings of inadequacy and failure. Whatever the intent of the individual who takes their own life, those left behind often interpret the act in ways that multiply their pain exponentially.[9]

In this chapter, we'll explore how guided imagery can offer a path to healing for those grappling with the aftermath of a loved one's suicide. Through the stories of Linda, Trevor, and Wendy, we'll witness the transformative power of this technique in addressing the unique challenges posed by suicide bereavement.

---

9   Hutton, D. (2023, September 8). Expert untangles complexities of grief for suicide loss survivors. CU Anschutz News. news.cuanschutz.edu/news-stories/expert-untangles-complexities-of-grief-for-suicide-loss-survivors

Linda's Story: Unraveling the Knots of Guilt and Resentment

Linda was the proud mother of three adult sons, all in their late thirties and early forties. She fondly recalled being close to all three gentlemen during their formative years and well into adulthood. An easygoing, generous, and accommodating woman, Linda took pride in her boys' accomplishments and made it a point to be their "go-to person," especially in the wake of her divorce from their biological father, Henry, when the boys were in their twenties.

It was Linda who filed for divorce, citing a history of physical and verbal abuse that largely occurred behind closed doors, outside the earshot of their children. Linda made two conscious decisions in an effort to protect her sons:

1. The boys must never know about Henry's abusive behavior. She reasoned that, overall, Henry was a good man who simply couldn't handle his liquor well. She made excuses for shiners, bumps, and bruises to shield the boys from their father's darker side.

2. No matter how bad things became, she would not divorce Henry while the children were growing up. Linda was determined that her boys would never be without a father, believing they loved and needed him, and that he adored all three of them.

Linda worked her plan, keeping the family intact until her youngest son, Jeff, graduated college at age twenty-two. She believed they were old enough, mature enough, and stable enough to weather the storm of divorce, especially since there had been little to no conflict in front of them.

Nine or ten months after Jeff's graduation, during a relatively peaceful period with no significant events on the family calendar, Linda filed for divorce. Henry, however, did not respond civilly to Linda's decision. He assumed the role of the blindsided victim, the man who had "broken his back" to feed, house, and clothe his family, only to be "discarded like an old pair of shoes" as soon as the last child left the house.

While Linda had guarded the boys from any disparaging information about their father, Henry launched a campaign to destroy Linda and her relationship with their sons. He told the boys that their mother never really loved him, had used him for his money, and was "nothing but a selfish taker." He even suggested that since she had been a stay-at-home mother throughout their childhood, "she must be screwing some new guy cause she ain't capable of making enough money herself to support that lifestyle."

Linda learned of Henry's legion of accusations, insults, and mockery from email exchanges with her oldest son, Ricky. It became clear that Henry was attempting to reprogram the boys to disregard their love and respect for their mother and replace it with disdain, painting her as the destroyer of their family who had "abandoned the boys for her selfish pursuits."

Henry's efforts were largely successful, at least with the two younger boys. He employed methods consistent with "parental alienation," a phenomenon coined by psychiatrist

Dr. Richard Gardner, suggesting that one parent attempts to destroy the bond between the child and the other parent.[10]

Ricky, however, remained steadfast in his devotion to his mother. "Mom," he said, "I could see right through Dad's lies. I know you love us—it's Dad you wanted to get away from. I have known you were unhappy for years."

Michael, the middle son, eventually "forgave" his mother, opting to be the "Switzerland kid" and maintaining a neutral stance that allowed him to potentially enjoy a relationship with both parents.

But Jeff, the youngest, remained estranged. The bridge between him and Linda was thoroughly burned, resulting in zero communication despite her earnest attempts to win him back through phone calls, emails, texts, and gifts. These desperate olive branches went unanswered as Jeff cut his mother off, maintaining a connection only with Henry and his brothers.

Gradually, Jeff distanced himself from Ricky, and then Michael. Then one day, after an ugly confrontation with his father where he blamed Henry for a myriad offenses as both a father and a husband, Jeff cut off the final member of his family of origin. Two weeks later, he was found hanging in his garage by local police after missing work for three consecutive days. There was no note, no explanation. He was twenty-eight years old.

---

10 Gardner, R. A. (1992). *The Parental Alienation Syndrome: A Guide for Mental Health and Legal Professionals.* Creative Therapeutics.

Linda's Guided Imagery Experience

Linda settled into my rocking chair, reclining just enough to relax and extend her legs, but not quite reaching a forty-five-degree angle. Her anxiety was palpable, but true to her word, she had decided to trust me. To my relief, she quickly complied with all the instructions in my relaxation induction, including inhaling to the count of three and exhaling to the count of five. Soon, her breathing deepened, and her eye movement conveyed that she was processing the narrative.

Typically, the greatest challenge of the guided imagery technique is ensuring the client's ability to experience the event—sight, sound, smell, and touch—as if it's actually happening. In Linda's case, she gave every indication that she was fully immersed in the experience. My only challenge now was to speak from her late son Jeff's vantage point, striving to sound as authentic as possible.

After a brief relaxation induction, I guided Linda to meet with Jeff in a place of her choosing. While I don't recall the exact location she chose (this session took place about a decade ago), I'll never forget what I said to Linda when speaking as Jeff:

> Mom, it's so good to see you. I feel like I just want to cry and cry. The pain that I have carried since the divorce, I don't even know how to communicate my feelings to you, but I will try. I'll never know what your marriage to Dad was like, but I never saw you guys fight. So I didn't see it coming. You know, the divorce, I mean. When you guys told me you were getting divorced, I

thought it was some kind of a joke. I mean, why was my family splitting up? At first it hit so hard, it was like I couldn't breathe and you just told me things like, "It was nobody's fault...and everything just fell apart... It'll be okay... We both love you very much... It'll be for the best, you'll see."

But then Dad told me bad things about you. He wondered whether you ever cared about anyone else besides yourself. Oh, and then he thought you were seeing someone else and I... Well, I just felt so betrayed, you know? I wanted to confront you with that, but I was embarrassed and I didn't know if it was true. And so, I did nothing. It was like I felt so abandoned by you, I couldn't trust you anymore. And Dad was saying terrible things to make you sound real bad and I didn't know what to believe. I felt sorry for him, but honestly I hated that he told me all of these terrible things about you not loving us and only caring about yourself. I felt sort of trapped, because he would ask me if I was talking to you and when I said no, he seemed relieved, you know? Like we were in this together, like teammates. At the same time, I felt guilty about not talking to you, but I just couldn't, because I knew he would feel so bad and he would give me a hard time.

So, the longer I didn't talk to you, the harder it was to pick up the phone and call you. And yes, I was really angry at you. I mean, if it wasn't anybody's fault, like you said, why did you have to do it, Mom? I was just so devastated and so lost, Mom, you know? I didn't know what to do. I just stopped caring about my job, my future career. I didn't want to date, because why bother? I felt alone and overwhelmed, and after a while I just felt hopeless. I wanted to reach out to you, but I just froze and gave up. And honestly, I was tired of Dad making me his sounding board... One day I was feeling just so depressed, with nothing to feel good about and nothing to look forward to. I was desperate. I just wanted to go to sleep and not wake up, Mom. I'm sorry. I couldn't take it anymore.

By this point, Linda was in tears, listening intently to my words spoken through Jeff. I paused, giving her the opportunity to respond to her son. Although she wasn't speaking aloud, I instructed her to say what she needed to say to Jeff, including:

Thank you for telling me your thoughts and feelings... I understand how hard that must have been for you. I'm so sorry, honey, I never meant to hurt you. You were always so precious to me, and part of the reason for that was your sweet sensitivity. I guess that's part of why the breaking of your family was so painful to you and why you took it so personally. If I knew these things at the time, I maybe could have done things differently. But we can't go back, I know that much. Are you okay where you are?

I spoke again for Jeff:

Oh yes, Mom, it's beautiful here and I'm well. There's no need to worry about me. But I want to make sure that you are okay. I guess I need to know that you understand what happened and most of all, that you forgive me. Will you please consider forgiving me, Mom?

Linda was nodding (while still crying a steady stream of tears) and responding very affirmatively to Jeff's request for forgiveness. I encouraged her to tell him:

Don't worry, Jeff, I will never resent you. I have forgiven you and will always love you. And I must also ask you, honey, will you please forgive me for how the divorce happened and how it hurt you? I didn't want to hurt you at all. In fact, I would have divorced your father a long time before then, but I wanted to wait until you three were old enough to experience a divorce and still be okay. But you know, if I knew then what I know now, I would have never put you through this, Jeff. I could have waited longer. I just didn't know you would be so devastated. I'm *so* sorry that you were hurt. But I'll tell you what. I just want us to forgive each other and find peace, if that's okay with you.

Linda nodded to assert that she could assimilate my instructions into her communication with Jeff. (I always ask my patients to communicate by raising their right index finger to affirm and the left one to disagree or negate.)

She raised her right index finger to also indicate that it was indeed her wish to forgive Jeff, to be forgiven by him, and then allow him to resume his life in the next realm.

Soon thereafter, I afforded her the opportunity to say goodbye to Jeff, as she was ready to release him, having nothing else to share, no other questions to ask, and nothing else to hear from Jeff's perspective. I brought Linda back to my office and back to her life in the here and now. As is almost always the case, she was relaxed and mostly silent; that just seems to be how people return from their imagery experiences.

But the next session is when I can normally tell if the procedure made a difference for the patient, in this case, Linda. She wasted no time informing me that the burden of guilt she carried regarding Jeff had been removed. She felt a lightness that he was okay, and no longer in such severe pain. She was able to forgive herself, especially because she acknowledged that she had done the best she could. The notion that her son was in the hands of the divine was very satisfactory to her, and certainly promoted greater peace.

In fact, the only thing that she admitted she was still carrying one week post-guided imagery was some resentment toward her ex-husband for the many crimes she charged him with. (And yes, the imagery may certainly have exacerbated that resentment.) But it was quickly and easily taken care of, as I challenged Linda to release that contempt toward him, as it was her poison that would bleed upon the other two boys in their efforts to heal from not only the divorce, but Jeff's suicide as well. Linda decided that a second guided imagery to address her ex-husband was not necessary, choosing letter writing (another Gestalt technique) to say her piece to him and then release him along with her resentment.

Linda has graduated from therapy. But as of last contact, some three years ago, and seven years post-guided imagery, she was still at peace with Jeff's suicide.

The Takeaway

Linda was grappling with several issues related to her son's death:

1. She missed him deeply.

2. She didn't know why he took his life, as he cut off communication and left no note.

3. She was hurting to think that he suffered silently while she felt powerless.

4. She was angry that she had learned that her ex was deliberately poisoning their children's minds to induce them to blame and punish her for divorcing him.

5. She felt that the suicide had left things utterly broken, with no direction and no closure.

My part in this process may be controversial to some people because I created words for her late son. However, my words seemed consistent with what she reported to me, including the following:

- Linda and Jeff were very close before the divorce.
- He was her most sensitive child.
- Henry was bad-mouthing Linda to the boys.
- Jeff cut his mother off from all communication.
- Jeff continued a relationship with Henry.
- Linda was seeking a peaceful resolution, not revenge.

- Linda learned from her other boys that Jeff was struggling with depression.
- No other information existed to confirm or contradict my words.

In other words, I used the facts and perspectives available to me to create a narrative that sounded plausible to me and, more importantly, to Linda. This "poetic license" assumed by the trusted therapist, I believe, should be predicated upon understanding the situation and the personalities involved, wherever possible. For instance, I will not involve the notion of an afterlife with patients who are atheists or believe that all life ceases at the end of a lifetime on Earth. (As noted last chapter, guided imagery can still be done, but the narrative should be altered to fit the patient's belief system.)

Was my iteration of Jeff's thoughts and feelings even remotely close to the truth? We will never know. But ultimately, this procedure is not about accuracy. It's not to be evaluated as factual, as might be done in a courtroom. The sole purpose of this interaction is to provide peace and closure to the patient.

And in Linda's case, that's exactly what happened. According to her, she has been at peace with Jeff's death since the advent of the guided imagery procedure, with no regrets, regression, or relapse to the time prior to the intervention.

Here are Linda's words, written in a thank-you card to me several weeks after the guided imagery session:

> Dear friend:
>
> I am feeling so much better! My physician here (in Virginia) has reduced my antidepressant by half and [I] hope to get off it. My relationship with my husband is so much better. I think it's because I am nicer and feel better. We are so enjoying our time together. He thanked me this morning for our day together yesterday! I am feeling better even though we have lots of rain and cool weather. Thank you for working a miracle with me. Dealing with the death [Jeff's suicide] was a turning point. I really appreciate you counseling me and helping me. I am so grateful I found you and grateful for all your help.
>
> Wishing you well—with gratitude—Linda

The Angel on Trevor's Shoulder

One of the more delightful young people I've had the pleasure of connecting with since the pandemic was a twenty-three-year-old gentleman I'll call "Trevor." An only child, Trevor was born to a successful salesman father and a mother who was a disabled college professor suffering from a debilitating autoimmune disease. After several years of fighting a losing battle with her illness, Trevor's mother took her own life, approximately four years prior to our first meeting.

As noted in my file on Trevor, "Patient suffers from significant symptoms of anxiety and depression, including self-deprecatory thinking [fancy name for putting himself down a lot], dysphoria [fancy name for low mood], chronic worrying, inability to relax, sleep disturbance, and pessimism regarding the future."

Trevor was already a college graduate with a promising career in civil engineering, but to talk to him was neither joyful nor relaxing. He presented as a burdened young man, devoid of youthful exuberance. Handsome and well-spoken, with good hair and a diminutive stature, he reminded me of a young Michael J. Fox.

From the earliest indications, a substantial percentage of Trevor's dysphoria, anxiety, and self-blame stemmed from the leftover baggage of his mother's suicide. He was mired in guilt for not knowing that his mother was desperately considering ending her life. "I mean, I saw her that very day and had no clue," he lamented, haunted by the fact that she was on the brink of overdosing. What could he have done to save his mom? In fact, he wondered what he'd done to make her want to leave him forever.

But in reality, Trevor knew that his mother adored him, worshipped her only child. He knew he wasn't the cause of his mother's death. But the sting of it was the idea that she willfully chose to leave him—illness and all—without her maternal support and love for the rest of his life. It was close to impossible to feel good after her decision to "abandon" him, and after four years, he reportedly had made zero progress in terms of making peace with his mother's death.

In only our second session, I introduced him to the idea of guided imagery. He was curious about the technique and quite invested in feeling better. Since his father knew me from local interactions, Trevor was willing to trust me with my recommendation.

Trevor's Guided Imagery

High-anxiety Trevor responded immediately to the relaxation induction—something that never ceases to amaze me about most anxious patients—and related that he could see and experience his mother in another realm. He noted that she looked well, remarkably strong, and no longer decimated by her disability. This pleased Trevor, needless to say.

I began the dialogue, speaking for his mother (but again, he was instructed to hear the words as if they were emanating from his mother's lips):

> Oh, Trevor, it is so good to see you. My heart just wants to burst with excitement from seeing you! You look well, my dear son, but of course, I can see your sadness. Well, this is hard for me. I was a little nervous, but very excited to see you. I know I need to begin with an apology. I'm sorry, Trevor, truly sorry to have left you like that. I'm sure you must be hurt and angry that I just left without a word. That must hurt terribly. I know

nothing I could say could ever suffice, but if it's okay with you, I'd like to try to explain.

As you well know, I was in daily pain, severe pain. Pain that I couldn't escape unless I took enough of those damned opioids to numb me and separate me from all of my feelings. And then, they'd wear off and my pain would return with a vengeance. I hurt so, so bad, Trevor, but I couldn't figure out what to do. If I complained to your dad, I could see the strain on his face. He was so burdened by my sickness—I felt so guilty being a drain on him. He couldn't leave the house without feeling that he had left me to fend for myself, and that made him feel so guilty. He was stuck between trying to make a living to pay my medical bills and staying home to take care of me. Some choice— the proverbial rock and the hard place. Your father is such a lovely man, always caring and rarely a word of complaint. But I knew that this illness was sucking the life out of him.

Truthfully, Trevor, my illness was killing both of us, not just me. And I knew I was draining you, my son. Instead of college being the time of life to play and learn and experience carefree exploration, you were anchored to this house to make sure you saw me almost every day. Not much of a college experience, eh? And don't forget, as a college professor, I witnessed college kids living the lifestyle that I hoped you would have one day. But your college was muted by my illness and I knew that. I felt like the ball and chain on your life.

So, I made a decision to unburden you and your father. I needed to relieve all three of us from my illness. *So why didn't I say goodbye?*, you must be thinking. Well, truthfully, I thought about it. A lot. But I knew if I mentioned it, my shrink and your father would deem me to be suicidal (which, of course, I was), but that would only culminate in my being involuntarily locked up in the local nut house, more drugs and counseling and...I was done, Trevor.

I was done hurting. I was done moaning in the night, waking your poor father. I was done ruining every event, every holiday, every dinner out. Enough was enough! And honestly, I couldn't think of a better way to do it than to just leave one day when you were at school and Dad was at work. Please, please, please forgive me! I always loved you, Trevor, and I always will. But my disease destroyed me. I needed to die. Please understand.

At this point, I handed the reins over to Trevor to see if there was anything else he needed to ask his mom. Also, I asked him to say whatever he needed to express to her. My/her explanation, fortunately, answered most of his queries about how she could do such a thing to him and his dad. But he went one step further and said to his mom, "But how am I going to make it through this life without you?"

In the silence of his own mind, he heard something from her own lips. Something he created. Something he made her say. Something he absolutely needed to hear. "My dear son," she said, "I will always be with you. I will be the angel on your shoulder for the rest of your life."

I don't know what else she said to him in his imagery experience. It doesn't matter. That phrase, that designation of an omnipresent angel, was exactly what Trevor needed to hear. He was instantaneously lifted by this made-up conversation in his head. He knew this the very day of the completion of the imagery. And the next week he told me how his perspective had changed. Mom was still gone, but it was okay. Because in a way, she was not out of his life. She would be there watching him, guiding and directing him, rooting him on. The best and most loving angel ever, sitting atop his shoulder.

I still see Trevor, about once a month now. We work on career, social life, emotional growth, etc. But he's good with Mom.

The Takeaway

Trevor's experience with guided imagery highlights several key points:

1. **The power of reframing:** By reimagining his mother as an "angel on his shoulder," Trevor was able to transform his perception of her absence from abandonment to continued presence and support.

2. **The importance of understanding:** Hearing his mother's explanation (even if imagined) helped Trevor make sense of her actions and alleviate his guilt.

3. **The healing potential of forgiveness:** The imagery work provided a space for mutual forgiveness, allowing Trevor to release his anger and hurt.

4. **The role of continued support:** While the guided imagery session was transformative, ongoing therapy has helped Trevor apply his new perspective to other areas of his life.

5. **The mind's capacity for healing:** Trevor's ability to generate the comforting image of his mother as an angel demonstrates the mind's innate ability to find solutions to emotional pain.

Trevor's story reminds us that sometimes, the most powerful healing comes not from changing the facts of what happened, but from changing how we perceive and carry those facts with us. The guided imagery provided a tool for Trevor to rewrite his narrative in a way that allowed him to move forward while maintaining a positive connection to his mother's memory.

Wendy's Story: Finding Peace After Tragedy

The holiday season in Western society often serves as a marker of time, especially when it comes to loss. You might hear someone say, "This is only the third Christmas since Grandpa passed," or, "This is the first holiday season without her beloved husband." Consequently, a time that's meant to be joyous and celebratory can instead become a period of despair, pronounced loneliness, and isolation.

For Wendy, Christmas 2021 became the single worst day of her life. After visiting with family, exchanging gifts, and celebrating the holiday, she and her husband, Randy, stumbled upon a point of heated disagreement. Both had reportedly drunk excessively that evening, allowing an unbridled flow of nasty exchanges between them.

Shortly after they arrived home, Wendy said one more thing that Randy didn't like. Relying on his alcohol-induced impaired judgment, he grabbed a nine-millimeter, walked into his office, and, without saying a word, took his own life.

Wendy was horrified to find him lying motionless on the floor of their bedroom. Predictably, she experienced a range of painful emotions: horror and shock, devastation, sadness, guilt, self-deprecation, pity for him, and rage toward him—all enveloped in a blanket of deep despair and hopelessness.

To me, Wendy was a friend of a friend, who later became my house cleaner, and eventually a platonic friend before she relocated to her home state of Ohio. She had been in a relationship with Randy for six and a half years, married for a year and a half, and was remarkably close to his children. Her own two kids had already left the nest and begun their own lives. In other words, Randy and his family had become the center of her world.

Wendy returned to Sarasota shortly after her husband's death, as she was wont to do every year to visit old friends.

We had lunch a time or two, as she admittedly wanted to pick my brain for any useful morsels of hope I could offer her after such a life-altering tragedy. Of course, I knew the right things to say—I'm eighty thousand hours into this gig as a psychologist. At the same time, I knew offering her confidence, reassurance, and support was helpful, but a long way from curative. Mostly, I just listened. I knew of her relationship with Randy. She told me of the challenges she had with him, especially his depression and alcohol abuse. Nonetheless, she described him as a good man, a faithful partner, and a hard worker.

Wendy returned to Florida this past February, just over two years after Randy's suicide. A group of us went out to dinner, and she and I got to talking about her ongoing struggle. She shared some of the unanswered questions she harbored, including "Didn't he love me?" and "Was this all my fault?"

We also discussed the technique of guided imagery, something I thought might be helpful to her, especially with her aforementioned questions and self-torment. She told me that her therapist in Ohio was not inclined to use that type of technique. She then asked if I would be willing to attempt it with her, as she already knew me and trusted me without reservation.

It's well-known in the field of psychology that licensed professionals are not supposed to treat family and/or friends. It's one of the cardinal rules. But I decided that the potential rewards of facilitating this technique dramatically exceeded the risk in doing so. I told her we would have her over Sunday evening for pasta, and I could facilitate a guided imagery session right before dinner.

Wendy's Guided Imagery Experience

Late Sunday afternoon, Wendy lay down upon my couch and allowed me to induce a mild state of relaxation using a progressive tension and release procedure. (I'll explain in more depth later in the book on how to conduct a guided imagery session.)

I received permission from Wendy to go to a place in her mind where she might be able to see Randy and create a meaningful dialogue with her late husband. She would be seeing him face-to-face in her imagery, and I would be contributing to the dialogue by speaking for Randy.

Wendy elected to speak her experience aloud, which allowed me to understand where her struggles lay and address those particular issues by responding as Randy might.

After the relaxation induction, I asked her to walk down a hallway and open the door to her right. This door led to the couple's living room, where Randy was seated and preparing himself to address his heartbroken wife.

Needless to say, all of this was created in Wendy's mind/ imagination, and I began to speak as Randy only when she told me that she had entered the room and could envision him. (Once again, being able to see and experience what is being described is arguably the most important part of guided imagery, and that which, in my history, is most predictive of a successful outcome.)

I offered Wendy the option of standing several feet from Randy, or if preferred, melting into his arms. She chose the latter, as she very much loved and missed him, and seeing him invoked an emotional reaction, making holding him an attractive option.

I followed that lead and gave them a couple of moments of an emotional embrace, although I told her that he was whispering, "I'm sorry. I'm so sorry," in her ear. She was clearly weeping at this point, and I had already prepared her with a box of Kleenex at her side and several tissues in her hand.

It did not take long for Wendy to conjure up a barrage of important, unanswered questions for Randy. (Recall that the technique of guided imagery is about helping people to finish that which is unfinished in their minds.) Wendy began to shower Randy with several of these questions, as she was stuck on these undigested items, preventing her from successfully progressing toward a healthy acceptance of Randy's death.

As Randy, I responded to the question, "How could you do this to me?" by again apologizing, stating, "I can't tell you how sorry I am. I was very drunk and not thinking rationally. I was very angry and hurt and thought that this would be the best way to shut off the pain."

Randy was not actively religious, but he did have respect for a higher being and believed in an afterlife. I blended this into my words, again speaking for Randy:

> I knew immediately that what I did was so wrong, but I could not undo it. There was a moment on the other side where I was actively pleading to return to the house and receive another chance to alter my decision. But essentially, I was told, "What's done is done."
>
> I want you to know, Wendy, that I am okay. In fact, I am quite well, having been forgiven for my stupid decision. The only thing that stands in the way of my being at peace here is worrying about you and the kids and wishing that you all could forgive me.

Wendy fired back passionately, "Didn't you love me?"

I (as Randy) responded quickly:

> Oh yes, with all of my heart. I always will. But it was me that I didn't love. Wendy, I know you know that I struggled throughout my life with a deep sense of inadequacy, and at times, real hatred of myself. You were truly the best thing that ever happened to me, but I could not easily accept your love, because I didn't feel worthy of it. It was very difficult for me sometimes, Wendy, because you loved me so much. You know I couldn't understand why or what you found to be so lovable, because I never found that in myself.

I'm sure you know that there were times when you were so good to me, but it made me very uncomfortable to be loved like that, so I would find ways to push you away, like finding something to be upset about to get some distance between us. I know that's not right. I wanted you to know that I appreciate your love more than I could ever let you know, but please understand that sometimes it made me so uncomfortable, because I never had anyone love me like that before.

So, I know I have no right to ask you this, but if there's any way you could find it in your heart to forgive me for that terrible thing I did, I would be truly grateful. I know I won't be around for anything in your life, and I know I won't be there for my kids anymore. I can't tell you how awful that feels to me, or how ashamed I am. I was such an idiot to do that. But Wendy, I really need you to forgive me. Do you think that maybe someday you would do that?

I paused a moment to ensure that Wendy had an opportunity to respond.

Wendy nodded tearfully, saying:

I forgive you, Randy, you stupid schmuck. I can't hate you; I can only hate what you did! But I am going to let go of that hatred right now and replace it with the memory of the most beautiful and passionate love I've ever had in my life for a man. You are one of the best things that has ever happened to me. I suppose that's why losing you hurts to this degree. But no more. I will release you to God's love and give myself the opportunity to finally find some peace. Goodbye, my love. Goodbye, my dear Randy.

Wendy's tears continued to flow at this point, as it became a reality that not only was Randy gone from this earth, but she was allowing and accepting that he would never be back for her.

Wendy made it clear to me that she had released him from her sight and he was now back to his celestial dwelling place, but without the extra baggage of horrible guilt and shame. The forgiveness that he sought from Wendy had been granted, willingly. Her forgiveness freed both of them from the ugliness of the suicide.

As is often the case, I asked my patient/participant to write about the experience as much as they could remember from the guided imagery session. These are Wendy's exact words about that experience.

In Wendy's Words

> I was in a relaxed and comfortable position on a sofa. Dr. Cortman slowly guided me down a long hallway, down a staircase to a movie theater. I was guided to be aware of the lighting of the theater, the smell of the theater, his presence, and the presence of the camera operator.
>
> Dr. Cortman pointed out the large screen in front of me and suggested I play the movie. The movie of my trauma and pain. My mind went to that night. I spoke of the

senseless argument my husband started. I saw him stop the car in the middle of the road and tell me he wanted a divorce. I asked him why he married me. I removed my wedding ring and threw it in the cup holder. I saw myself saying those final words, "Merry fucking Christmas." I then saw my husband walk into our house, walk past me in the kitchen and to his office. I then heard the sound of the ear-piercing gunshot.

I was in that horrible moment yet again, having relived it over and over for the last two years. Dr. Chris asked me if I had any questions of my husband. And the questions flew. "Why did you do this?" "Do you realize what you have done?" "Do you know how much I loved you?" "Did you love me?" "Are you sorry?"

To each and every question I had, Dr. Chris answered as if he were my husband. He answered every question exactly as I had hoped my husband would respond. Though I had begged and screamed these questions into space for two years, for the first time I received answers. "I'm so sorry I hurt you," "Yes, I love you," "I was in a bad place mentally and would take it all back if I could," "I'm so very sorry for the pain I've caused you."

I finally ran out of unanswered questions. I was guided to hold and kiss my husband for as long as I needed. This embrace, though empty, felt as though I was actually holding him, not wanting to let go. Just us together in that moment. I then said the thing that was the furthest from my mind: "I forgive you."

> Since my guided imagery I have felt like a huge weight was lifted from me, a closure of the intense pain and misery. I can now breathe. I now look forward to a life when I had lost all hope and direction. I can now be happy without guilt for doing so. While forgiving my husband, I found that I have also forgiven myself.
>
> Will I miss him? Of course. Will I still become sad? Of course. I now also know that there is a beautiful life that I had been missing. I no longer think of taking my own life. I have much to be thankful for and much more life to live.
>
> Mission accomplished!

At the time of this writing, six months after the guided imagery session, Wendy has a new lease on life. While she lost Randy, she has regained Wendy. There are no more thoughts of taking her own life to join him. Gone is the belief that her life is meaningless without him. She now recognizes that, even without him, she has much to live for. In fact, her biological grandson just landed a football scholarship at a Division One school. This is even more exciting for Wendy, as prior to his signing a letter of intent, she had suffered a lifetime as a loyal Cleveland Browns fan.

The Takeaway

So how did this technique work so powerfully? First and foremost, the procedure, although completely imaginary, became reality to her as she could see, hear, touch, and smell her husband as if he were in the room with her. Holding onto him was experienced, again, as if Randy had appeared in vivo.

In other words, the entire procedure was experienced as reality, and as a fact, not as imagination. Evidently, her nervous system accepted this experience as real. My words—spoken through Randy—provided her with exactly what she needed to let this go. To wit:

- Yes, he loved her.
- Yes, it was his own stupid and impulsive decision.
- No, it was not something that she caused or deserved.
- Yes, he had deeper issues of inadequacy.
- Yes, because he was drunk, he was incapable of rational decision-making at that moment.
- Yes, he was sorry and regretted his decision.
- And yes, he loved her very much and missed her as much as she missed him.

All of this combined to empower Wendy to release Randy to a heavenly forever, where he could be forgiven, at peace, finally without the turmoil that had contributed to so many of the squabbles and conflicts that the couple experienced in their decade of being together.

Wendy could now place Randy in a positive place in her mind, knowing that he was okay, would continue to be okay, and that she needed to do nothing more, as she had forgiven him and he was now in God's capable hands. She could now shift her focus to honoring him by loving his children and promoting them in their pursuits. She could also give herself permission to live her own life without the burden of worrying about a man who had painful and unresolved issues. Finally, she could allow herself to feel some relief, knowing that she had loved successfully and had been loved with that same fiery passion.

And now that relationship was over, despite the fact that both people would continue to love each other for eternity.

Conclusion: The Healing Power of Guided Imagery in Suicide Bereavement

As we've seen through the stories of Linda, Trevor, and Wendy, guided imagery can be a powerful tool in helping individuals process and find peace after losing a loved one to suicide. This technique offers several unique benefits:

1. **Providing Closure:** Guided imagery allows individuals to have the conversations they never got to have, addressing unfinished business and unanswered questions.

2. **Reframing the Loss:** By creating new narratives around the suicide, individuals can find ways to make meaning out of their loss and reframe their relationship with the deceased.

3. **Facilitating Forgiveness:** The technique provides a safe space for both forgiving the deceased and self-forgiveness, crucial steps in the healing process.

4. **Addressing Guilt and Self-Blame:** Through imagined dialogues, survivors can address and often alleviate

feelings of guilt and self-blame that are common in suicide bereavement.

5. **Creating Continuing Bonds:** As seen in Trevor's story, guided imagery can help create positive, ongoing connections with the deceased that support healing rather than hinder it.

6. **Emotional Catharsis:** The vivid, emotionally charged nature of the experience allows for a deep release of pent-up emotions.

7. **Personalized Healing:** Because the imagery is generated by the individual's own mind, the experience is uniquely tailored to their needs and beliefs.

While guided imagery is not a magic solution, and often works best as part of a comprehensive therapeutic approach, these stories demonstrate its potential to catalyze significant shifts in how individuals relate to their loss. By providing a bridge between the world of the living and their imagined connection with the deceased, guided imagery offers a unique path toward healing and acceptance.

As we move forward, it's crucial to remember that each person's journey through grief is unique, and what works for one may not work for all. However, the power of imagination, when harnessed with compassion and clinical insight, can open doors to healing that many might have thought forever closed.

Chapter Seven

Treating Sleep Issues with Guided Imagery

I found myself on a cruise recently, not in pursuit of rest and relaxation, but in search of material for this book. During my voyage, I encountered a licensed mental health counselor from the Dallas area. When I mentioned I was writing a book on guided imagery, she nodded knowingly, explaining that she was familiar with the technique and its applications in helping people relax, reduce anxiety, and improve sleep. She was absolutely right, of course, but if those were the only benefits of guided imagery, this book would never have been written.

While the counselor's understanding of guided imagery was accurate, it barely scratched the surface of this powerful technique's potential. That said, I have indeed used guided imagery specifically for sleep disorders, and I'd like to share a couple of particularly illuminating cases.

Virginia's Story: Finding Peace in the Sand

Virginia was a survivor of what I would characterize as ninety-ninth percentile childhood abuse. Her recollections included horrific incidents, such as a grandmother who, among other atrocities, reportedly threw kittens into the fireplace to hear them scream.

Virginia's PTSD symptoms were textbook for someone with her traumatic history. She experienced the typical repetition of traumatic incidents and avoidance of any reminders of her particular experiences. For instance, given the horrors she was exposed to in childhood, Virginia sought to minimize her exposure to anything involving blood or depictions of blood. As a result, she was unable to take communion in her Protestant church.

Many of Virginia's traumatic memories involved being awakened at night and subjected to her grandmother's sadistic practices. Like many survivors of childhood trauma I've worked with, she had essentially learned to sleep with one eye open, developing a hypervigilance that is a hallmark symptom of PTSD. While we didn't determine the exact impact on her sleep stages and depth, it was clear that Virginia had endured many years of subpar sleep.

She was easily disturbed by the proverbial "things that go bump in the night" and was all but paralyzed by the thunder and lightning storms that are staples of Florida summers, their explosive nature reminiscent of incoming artillery.

Years of insufficient sleep and an inability to reach the deepest levels of rest eventually caught up with Virginia. She was perpetually tired, irritable, restless, disinterested, and prone to nodding off during any sedentary task.

Unsurprisingly, we had her physician confirm a sleep disorder diagnosis. He wanted to prescribe a benzodiazepine, a tranquilizing medication to be used as needed. That was her physician's job. Mine was to help her reduce her hypervigilance, learn to relax, and let go.

We recorded a guided imagery session for Virginia to use nightly. The session began with about ten minutes of deep breathing exercises, giving her permission to release anything troubling her and embrace the positive aspects of her life and faith. For instance, Virginia was encouraged to focus on gratitude that she had not only survived a terrible childhood, but was now living a happy and successful life. This life included a strong, committed, and stable husband, a thriving family business, and "two easy-to-raise sons, destined for their own success."

As part of the relaxation process, I guided Virginia down a flight of stairs in her mind, with each step representing a deeper descent into relaxation until we reached the bottom floor. As I often do, I had her walk down a hallway until she reached a door on her right. Opening that door would lead her to the most beautiful and relaxing place in the world for her. She chose Siesta Beach, often touted as one of the best beaches in the country, if not the world. The incredibly soft, powdery white sand is reportedly 99 percent quartz and 100 percent easy on the feet, even during the blistering days

Treating Sleep Issues with Guided Imagery

of a Southwest Florida summer. (There's my Chamber of Commerce moment for Sarasota, Florida.)

In the imagery, we had Virginia walk to a secluded spot on the beach. She brought suntan lotion, a big straw hat, and sunglasses reminiscent of Elton John's more flamboyant days. With her comfortable beach chair and feet nestled in the warm surf, she was ready to relax—and sleep.

This scenario represented peace for Virginia: no interruptions, no interactions with people, and no psychotic grandmother. Just rest and relaxation. Unlike the other guided imagery exercises in this book, which are typically one-time experiences, Virginia used this recording nightly to help her fall asleep.

When she woke up in the middle of the night, as most of us over forty tend to do, she had the option of playing it again. Virginia reported that she rarely reached the part of the recording where her toes were submerged in the Gulf of Mexico because she would be asleep by that point in the procedure.

Within months, Virginia no longer needed to play the recording. She could simply close her eyes and begin the process without my voice, often skipping over the relaxation part in favor of heading straight to Siesta for, well, a siesta.

But the recording was always there if necessary, which represented a form of security for Virginia—a concept especially important to her, given her childhood filled with scary and disturbing experiences.

To this day, Virginia remains a good sleeper with a predictable bedtime, good sleep hygiene, and mostly pleasant dreams—all indications of a sound and stable mindset.

The Alligator on the Green: Jared's Story

I don't know many twelve-year-olds who have sleep disorders. As of this writing, I have a twelve-year-old son who approximates a sleep disorder only because he can sleep for eighteen straight hours if allowed. Miraculously, from an aging father's perspective, he doesn't need to get up to pee even once during the night.

But twelve-year-old Jared was brought to see me by his mother because he was not sleeping well at all. In fact, his sleep was so poor that he had resorted to sleeping on the living room couch. He had evicted himself from his own bedroom for a reason unknown to his loving parents.

It's always important for a clinician to ascertain when any particular symptom first appeared and what circumstances may have been involved. Jared was embarrassed to admit it to me, but he knew exactly when, how, and why he lost his ability to sleep.

"I saw a movie recently," he said sheepishly, "and the boy in the movie found a dead girl under his bed. But she wasn't just lying there, she was talking to him."

"Do you mean *The Sixth Sense*?" I inquired.

Jared smiled broadly. "Yes. Exactly."

"Your parents let you watch that one, I guess?" This was a deliberate question on my part to reassure him that he had done nothing wrong, but was likely a little too young to digest the notion of talking to dead people, especially when they're inclined to hang out under your bed.

I made plans with Jared for a follow-up session where we would do a guided imagery exercise. I needed time to think about how I was going to direct our little "movie" to put away his unfortunate preoccupation with dead people. My office manager found a spot for him the very next day, so I had to think quickly about the best way to handle this.

When Jared returned, he knew we were going to do some type of procedure with his eyes closed and imagining things. He was fine with that. I asked if he wanted to imagine having a meeting with Bruce Willis, the star of the movie. All he would need to do was imagine Mr. Willis in his mind, and I would do the talking for him. That sounded like a plan to Jared.

He was remarkably easy to relax, quickly melting into the La-Z-Boy chair. Perhaps that was because he wasn't getting much sleep at home. I decided to give him the option of either talking to Mr. Willis face-to-face in a meeting spot, or keeping the actor on the big screen and having them discuss things while Jared was sitting in his favorite movie theater, next to me.

He chose the latter. We headed to Hollywood 20, his favorite theater. I handed him an imaginary remote and let him know that when he hit the play button, Bruce Willis would be on the screen ready to talk to him. I made certain that he could see, feel, and experience all aspects of this, as it was necessary, of course, that everything be as real as possible.

He gave me the signal that he was ready to begin, and I told him that Mr. Willis was on the big screen ready to speak to him. He immediately raised his right index finger to affirm that he saw the actor on the big screen. I began as Bruce:

> Hey Jared, I'm Bruce Willis. It's nice to meet you. I heard that you had a chance to see my movie, right?

I could see Jared nodding his head.

> Well, come here. I want to show you some things on the set of the movie. First of all, you understand that this is a movie and everything is fake, right? Remember when I got shot at the beginning of the movie? Well, I didn't really get shot, and I didn't die. I'm still alive, just like you.

I could see Jared smiling.

> And you see this stuff? This is ketchup, not blood. Look, I'm gonna squirt some on my hands and on my shirt. I can't believe I just poured ketchup on my new shirt for you, Jared.

More smiling from Jared.

Look here, I got someone I wanna introduce you to. This is Mischa, the little girl that was under the bed. Look at her. Does she look scary to you?

Jared was embarrassed to admit, "No."

I had the little girl say hi to Jared and apologize for scaring him. (I think I saw him blush at this time.) I had her continue:

I am only an actress, and I am not scary. It's really just a job that I did for the movie. Everyone here is so nice to me. Please don't worry about me, I'm actually very nice.

I gave Jared time to speak to Mr. Willis and Mischa in the silence of his head, and I challenged him to ensure that he would never be afraid of them or that movie again. I had him tell them that he was going back to his room to reclaim his bed and his status as an excellent sleeper.

Moments later, we left the theater, and I returned Jared to my office. He opened his eyes and said straightaway, "There's a giant alligator on the golf course!"

I admittedly worried for a second that somehow I had put a twelve-year-old kid with a sleep issue into a psychotic state. "That can't be. Maybe you're just still in imaginary land?"

"Nope, not imagining. Come see for yourself."

I got up from my chair, walked over to the window overlooking the golf course, and saw what must have been a fourteen-foot alligator on the putting green. That had never happened before or since. I blame Jared.

I never needed to see him after that session. His mother called, admitting embarrassment over letting him see the movie in the first place, but also to reassure me that he was back in his room, sleeping like a twelve-year-old should.

Conclusion: The Power of Imagination in Overcoming Sleep Issues

These two cases, while vastly different in their origins and manifestations, highlight the versatility and effectiveness of guided imagery in treating sleep disorders. Whether dealing with deep-seated trauma or childhood fears, the technique allows individuals to create new, positive mental associations that can replace anxiety and hypervigilance with relaxation and peace.

For Virginia, the guided imagery provided a safe, tranquil mental space that allowed her to gradually let go of her hypervigilance and sink into restful sleep. The beach scene became a powerful tool for relaxation, one that she could eventually access without the recording, demonstrating the lasting impact of well-crafted guided imagery.

Jared's case shows how guided imagery can be used to directly address and reframe the source of sleep disturbances. By "meeting" the actors from the movie that had frightened him and seeing behind the scenes, Jared was able to separate fantasy from reality and overcome his fear.

In both cases, the key was creating vivid, personalized mental experiences that felt real to the individuals. This underscores one of the fundamental principles of guided imagery: what the mind can conceive and believe, it can achieve. By harnessing the power of imagination, we can create new mental pathways that lead to better sleep and overall well-being.

While these examples focus on sleep issues, they hint at the broader potential of guided imagery in addressing a wide range of psychological and physiological concerns. As we continue to explore this technique, we'll see how it can be adapted to tackle various challenges, always with the goal of empowering individuals to tap into their own mental resources for healing and growth.

Chapter Eight

Guided Imagery and Miscellaneous Applications

When you conjure an image of a surfer, what springs to mind? Perhaps you envision sun-bronzed teenagers with salt-tousled hair, their vocabulary a colorful tapestry of "dude," "stoked," and the occasional "gnarly." What likely doesn't materialize in your mind's eye is Kerri: a fifty-year-old college professor with two adult children and a wrinkly Shar-Pei as a faithful companion.

Yet here was Kerri, her intellectual curiosity and zest for life as boundless as the ocean she was about to challenge, deciding to take up surfing of all pursuits. It's not typically the kind of endeavor people embark upon in their fifth decade, any more than they might try out for the NFL or take up professional ballet. But there she was, poised to "hang ten" alongside her husband, James, a seasoned surfer whose glory days harked back to the sun-soaked '70s.

Kerri's Story: When Waves of Trauma Meet the Shores of Recovery

Fate, it seems, has a cruel sense of irony. It was on Kerri's very first attempt to catch a wave that disaster struck. As she recounted the harrowing tale in our session, I could almost feel the sickening impact of her head against the ocean floor, an experience I'd had a taste of myself, albeit less drastically, while body surfing years ago.

The cracking of vertebrae, the shock of realization, the involuntary inhalation of saltwater, being yanked from the ocean's grip by a frantic James—Kerri's neck and back screaming in protest, her vocal cords joining the agonized chorus. In those interminable moments, as the line between life and death blurred like the horizon in a storm, Kerri grappled with a chilling question. If she survived, would a wheelchair be her lifelong companion?

Nine months had passed since that fateful day when Kerri first crossed my threshold. In what could only be described as a minor miracle, she was already bicycling, walking, lifting weights, and attending yoga classes, her prognosis promising a near-complete recovery. But while her body below the neck was on a trajectory of healing, her mind remained trapped in the tumultuous waves of that traumatic day.

Night after night, Kerri found herself jolted awake, gasping for air, terror coursing through her veins as vivid as it had been on that ill-fated day. In her dreams, she relived the crash with excruciating detail—the head-slamming impact, the suffocating sensation of drowning, the paralyzing fear of a life confined to a wheelchair. Each night, this torment played out like a sadistic movie on repeat.

"Why?" she implored me, her eyes searching for answers. "Why does this nightmare persist when my body is healing, when my prognosis is so promising? If I'm on the path to recovery, what purpose do these dreams serve?"

Her questions, though unique to her experience, echoed a familiar refrain I'd heard countless times in my practice. It's not uncommon for mental health professionals to encounter individuals grappling with recurrent, traumatic dreams— dreams that force them to revisit an unprocessed horror show, a story without a satisfying conclusion. I've witnessed this pattern in first responders haunted by the scenes they've encountered, in combat veterans reliving the horrors of war, in survivors of incest unable to escape their past, and in those who've lived through catastrophic accidents.

These nightmares, along with flashbacks and intrusive recollections, form the unholy trinity of post-traumatic stress disorder (PTSD) symptoms. In Kerri's case, while her physical body was making remarkable strides toward recovery, her mind remained a prisoner to one of the most terrifying moments of her life. The recurring dream, with its focus on the most frightening aspects of the accident—the loss of control, the head impact, the near-drowning, and the specter of lifelong disability—was her psyche's way of grappling with unresolved trauma.

The arsenal of treatments for PTSD is diverse. Sometimes, the most basic form of talk therapy, where the patient recounts the traumatic event and its associated emotions, is sufficient to help them move past the painful memory. In other cases, more specialized approaches are necessary. These might include eye movement desensitization and reprocessing (EMDR), a technique that helps the brain reprocess traumatic memories; rapid response therapy (RRT), which aims to quickly neutralize the emotional charge of traumatic experiences; prolonged exposure (PE), which gradually helps individuals confront their fears; or even the seemingly simple act of journaling or writing letters about the incident, allowing for emotional release and cognitive processing.[11]

But for Kerri, I had a different approach in mind, one that the astute reader of this book might have already anticipated: guided imagery. Given my history of working with several members of her family, Kerri didn't hesitate to place her trust in me when I proposed this intervention. I assured her that there was a good chance we could finally put her recurring nightmare to rest.

The following week, Kerri returned, a mix of anticipation and apprehension visible in her eyes. My plan was to begin with a five- to ten-minute relaxation induction, a crucial preparatory step. Then, we would embark on a journey to a metaphorical movie theater in her mind. There, Kerri would be given control—a remote control, to be precise—allowing her to navigate the playback of her surfing accident on the big screen of her imagination.

---

11 Rivia Mind. (n.d.). What are the different types of traumas? riviamind.com/types-of-traumas

I emphasized to Kerri that she held the power in this scenario. She could pause, fast-forward, or even stop the mental film entirely if it became too overwhelming. The goal was to give her complete agency over the traumatic memory that had held her captive for so long.

Kerri, ever the exemplary student (she had once invited me to give a guest lecture on stress in one of her classes), took to the exercise with remarkable aptitude. She complied swiftly and fully with the relaxation component of the imagery. Before long, she signaled with her right index finger—our pre-arranged sign—indicating that she could vividly see, hear, smell, and feel herself in the imaginary theater.

What unfolded next was a powerful and emotional journey. Kerri, armed with her mental remote control, pressed play and watched the surfing accident unfold on the screen of her mind, from start to finish. She felt anew the paralyzing helplessness and terror as the merciless undertow dragged her to the ocean floor. Tears welled up and spilled over as she relived the concussive blow and the searing pain that radiated from her neck throughout her body. The floodgates opened further as she witnessed James's frantic efforts to pull her from the water's deadly embrace, an act that likely saved her from drowning.

The crescendo of her emotional release came as she confronted the terrifying moment when she feared paralysis, unable to feel or move her extremities. The scene continued to unfold, culminating in the arrival of the EMTs—an unexpected touch of levity as Kerri recalled their attempts to flirt with her, eliciting her first smile since the ordeal began.

As the mental film concluded, Kerri hit the stop button, having experienced the trauma in its entirety. But our work wasn't done. I encouraged her to take an extraordinary step—to enter the movie scene herself and offer comfort and encouragement to the Kerri on the screen. This self-comforting exercise allowed her to remind herself of her resilience, her survival, and the excellent prognosis that awaited her. It was a powerful way to reframe the experience, infusing hope and optimism into a memory that had been dominated by fear and despair.

When Kerri returned to the present moment in my office, she was visibly drained, the emotional toll of reliving her trauma evident in her demeanor. Yet, beneath the exhaustion, there was an unmistakable sense of peace, a palpable relief that this experience was now behind her. Only time would tell if this sense of resolution would persist, but the initial signs were promising.

Kerri's own recollection of the experience, which she later shared with me, confirmed the profound impact of the guided imagery session.

> The main thing I remember is that you really wanted me to be specific and include every detail, "no matter how small," and lots of sensory stuff. And then you said you'd be sitting right next to me in the movie theater and to imagine it was playing for a one-night-only show and when it (I) was finished, now I had the power to decide what to do with the DVD of the movie: shred it, burn it, or save it on my computer. I saved it but have not looked at it since, even when I emailed it to you.

> Yes, the guided imagery you had me do helped me tremendously, as I never had the recurring nightmare again about my surfing accident. Remember when you told me that it was going to play in a movie theater for one night only and then I could decide what to do with my written narrative? Well, that painful experience is exactly where it belongs, forever laid to rest in the past. Thank you!

The success of this guided imagery session can be attributed to several factors. Kerri was given the opportunity to experience every painful, frightening, and traumatic aspect of her accident, but this time with a crucial difference—she was in control. She was the director of her own mental movie, empowered with the ability to navigate and, importantly, to stop the playback. This sense of agency was something she lacked during the actual traumatic event.

Moreover, the exercise allowed Kerri to demonstrate to herself that she no longer needed to live in fear of this recurring nightmare. By facing it head-on in a controlled, supportive environment, she was able to process the experience and, ultimately, let it go.

The proof of the technique's efficacy has stood the test of time. Seven years have passed since our guided imagery session, and Kerri reports not a single recurrence of the nightmare or flashback to the event. In this case, a single session of guided imagery succeeded where months of natural healing had not, freeing Kerri from the grip of her traumatic memory and allowing her to fully embrace her physical recovery.

Doug's Anxiety: An Unexpected Journey to Peace

In my years of practice, the transformative power of guided imagery has never ceased to amaze me. Time and again, I've witnessed remarkable healing unfold in a single session, particularly when addressing unresolved grief or trauma. Yet, Doug's story stands out as uniquely surprising, a testament to the technique's potential even a decade after our work together.

Doug first walked into my office ten years ago, a sixty-six-year-old man carrying a complex tapestry of symptoms. On the surface, he presented with mild to moderate depression— that familiar constellation of low mood, anhedonia (the inability to find pleasure in once-enjoyable activities), a pessimistic outlook, and self-deprecating thoughts. Beneath this layer lurked marital issues: power struggles, verbal conflicts, and a noticeable lack of intimacy. But it was the third element of Doug's psychological trifecta that would prove most intriguing: generalized anxiety disorder (GAD).

GAD, for those unfamiliar, manifests as a persistent state of hyperarousal in the nervous system. It's anxiety incarnate—a constant companion of worry, edginess, and an inability to relax. Those grappling with GAD often find themselves caught in a cycle of sleep disturbances and irritability, their minds a ceaseless whirlwind of what-ifs and worst-case scenarios.

In our high-stress society, anxiety disorders have become the common cold of mental health, affecting more than

18 percent of the population. One might argue it's more surprising that nearly 82 percent don't meet the diagnostic criteria.[12] But Doug's case was unique—he could pinpoint the exact origin of his anxiety, tracing it back to a childhood ritual that had morphed into a lifelong burden.

As a boy of seven or eight, Doug's evenings followed a comforting pattern. His parents would tuck him in, a nightly ritual of kisses, hugs, and sometimes stories, always concluding with a warm "Good night. We love you! Now get some sleep!" It was a scene of domestic tranquility, the kind that forms the bedrock of childhood security.

But for Doug, this nightly comfort was short-lived. As soon as his parents left the room, a strange compulsion would take hold. He'd climb out of bed and scurry to his bedroom window, watching as his parents' car backed out of the driveway and disappeared into the night. This departure left Doug alone with his older brother, Steve—a presence that should have been reassuring, but was instead a source of dread.

Steve, five years Doug's senior, was not the protective older sibling of storybooks. Instead, he was a tormentor, never hesitating to pick on Doug, mock him, or assert his dominance through bullying. In Doug's young mind, his parents' nightly departure wasn't just a temporary absence— it was the vanishing of all adult protection, leaving him vulnerable in a suddenly threatening world.

---

12 Cortman, C., Shinitzky, H., & O'Connor, R. (2014). *Take Control of Your Anxiety: A Drug-Free Approach to Living a Happy, Healthy Life.* Career Press.

This nightly vigil at the window marked the birth of Doug's anxiety. It's a textbook illustration of what I call the anxiety equation: investment plus perceived threat equals autonomic arousal.[13] In simpler terms, when we care deeply about something (in this case, Doug's own well-being) and perceive a threat to it (Steve's bullying), anxiety naturally follows.

Initially, Doug's anxiety was time-specific, beginning as he watched his parents drive away and lasting until the early morning hours when he finally felt safe enough to sleep deeply. But as often happens, this specific anxiety began to generalize. The challenges of elementary school—more bullying, academic struggles, social pressures—provided fertile ground for Doug's anxiety to grow and spread. What started as a nightly occurrence became a constant state of being. Doug had learned to be anxious around the clock.

In treating anxiety, psychologists often employ a two-pronged approach. The cognitive component involves learning to let go of what's beyond our control, while the behavioral aspect might include rigorous exercise, meditation, and relaxation techniques. We explored all of these avenues in Doug's treatment.

But as we worked together, a thought occurred to me. What if we could use guided imagery to address the root of Doug's anxiety—that childhood scene that had set this lifelong pattern in motion? It was a long shot, but with no risk to Doug, it seemed worth trying. To my surprise, Doug agreed without hesitation.

---

13 Cortman, C., Shinitzky, H., & O'Connor, R. (2014). *Take Control of Your Anxiety: A Drug-Free Approach to Living a Happy, Healthy Life.* Career Press.

What happened next was nothing short of remarkable. Despite his chronic anxiety, Doug moved into the relaxation component of the process with unexpected ease. His breathing slowed, and within minutes, his 6'2" frame became a study in stillness on my black leather couch.

I guided Doug to his favorite movie theater in his mind's eye, where we prepared to watch the childhood scene that had haunted him for so long. He saw his seven-year-old self being tucked in, then running to the window to watch his parents drive away. I asked him to fully experience the anxiety of that moment, to feel it as intensely as he had as a child. My goal was to help Doug reclaim control over his anxiety—to find the on/off switch, so to speak.

Then came the crucial moment. I asked adult Doug to enter the scene and introduce himself to his younger self. I encouraged him to impress upon little Doug how strong and capable he had become, to reassure the child that there was no longer any need for fear. In a touch of whimsy that felt right in the moment, I suggested that big Doug help little Doug find the "controls" for his anxiety—to turn down the volume as if it were a radio dial from the 1950s.

To my amazement, little Doug in the imagery not only found the knob but turned the anxiety down to nothing. He even practiced turning it on and off, demonstrating mastery over what had once controlled him. It seemed almost too simple, too good to be true.

But the imagery wasn't over. I invited Doug to create moments of joy and playfulness with his younger self, to experience the father-son bond that he had perhaps longed for. Doug spent over a minute in silent communion with his younger self, and when he indicated that he was ready, I asked him to merge the two versions of Doug into one healthy, non-anxious whole.

As Doug opened his eyes and returned to my office, he was quiet and relaxed, offering little more than that he felt "fine." I wondered if the session had made any real impact.

A week later, Doug returned with his usual list of topics to discuss. Almost as an afterthought, I asked about his anxiety. His response caught me off guard. He paused, looked inward for a moment, and then said with a note of surprise, "Funny, I haven't been thinking about it. But it seems like my anxiety is gone!"

I was stunned. Could one session really have dissolved decades of chronic anxiety? It seemed too good to be true, but I accepted it as fact, at least for the moment.

Over the following weeks and months, I periodically checked in about Doug's anxiety. "Any anxiety lately?" "Hey Doug, how's the anxiety?" "Have those anxiety symptoms ever surfaced?" Each time, his answer was the same: "Nope, no anxiety. Not since the imagery."

Doug continued therapy for a while to work on other aspects of his life—marital issues, questions of life purpose, challenges to his faith. But his anxiety, the constant companion of six decades, never returned.

How do we explain this seemingly miraculous transformation? While it's impossible to pinpoint the exact mechanism, it appears that Doug's guided imagery session allowed him to rewrite a core belief that had shaped his world for sixty years. In that therapeutic moment, Doug experienced the safety and reassurance of a powerful, competent adult—ironically, himself. This experience seemed to unlock a new sense of self-efficacy, a concept introduced by psychologist Albert Bandura.[14]

Self-efficacy is the belief in one's ability to handle whatever life throws our way. By changing this fundamental belief at a deep, experiential level, Doug was able to shed his clinical anxiety—the kind that's too frequent, too intense, and lasts far longer than necessary. He retained the natural capacity for appropriate anxiety in genuinely threatening situations, but the overwhelming, chronic anxiety that had defined much of his life was gone.

While Doug's experience may not be universal, it stands as a powerful testament to the potential of guided imagery. In just one session, he was able to overcome clinical anxiety that had persisted for more than half a century. It's a reminder of the mind's incredible capacity for change and healing, given the right tools and circumstances.

---

14 McLeod, S. (2023). Self-efficacy and social cognitive theories. Simply Psychology. simplypsychology.org/self-efficacy.html

The Bump in the Road: Hillary's Collision with Fate

In the tapestry of human experience that we, as therapists, are privileged to witness, certain threads appear with striking regularity. Unless you specialize in a niche area of psychology, you'll find that over 80 percent of your patients seek help for one of three issues: relationship problems (including challenges with children), anxiety, or depression.[15]

But there's a fourth category that, while less common, often presents some of the most profound challenges. These are the individuals who have experienced a trauma, catastrophe, or upset so significant that they simply can't move past it. Sometimes, it's a long-standing trauma, like Robert's World War II story we explored earlier. Other times, it's a more recent wound, raw and bleeding, like the one Hillary brought into my office.

Hillary was a twenty-seven-year-old reporter, divorced and childless, with a quick wit that could slice through tension like a hot knife through butter. Her intelligence was evident in every carefully chosen word, her vast knowledge a testament to a voracious appetite for reading. Her sense of humor was a perfect complement to mine, which, of course, endeared her to me immediately. (After all, any patient who laughs at my jokes is clearly of superior intellect and impeccable taste.)

But the issue that brought Hillary to my office was far from amusing. On a dark, deserted highway one night, Hillary's life

---

15 National Institute of Mental Health. (2022, September). Major depression. nimh.nih.gov/health/statistics/major-depression

changed in an instant when her car struck a sleeping, heavily intoxicated man on the road. It was one of those moments that divide life into "before" and "after," a stark reminder of how quickly our world can be turned upside down.

Hillary had been doing everything right. She was driving within a few miles of the speed limit, her attention focused on the road ahead, even wearing her prescribed glasses. But in the inky blackness of night, by the time the man's form became visible on the asphalt, it was already too late.

With trembling hands, Hillary pulled over to the shoulder and dialed 911. The highway stretched before her, dark and eerily empty. She knew it would be too dangerous to run onto the road to check on the man, so she remained by her car, tears streaming down her face as she prayed fervently that he would somehow be okay.

He wasn't. The emergency responders arrived with impressive speed, but their swift action couldn't change the grim reality. The man was pronounced dead at the scene. In a twist of fate that offered cold comfort, they assured Hillary it wasn't her fault. The man reeked of alcohol, a nearly empty bottle of Jack Daniels still clutched in his right hand, his blood alcohol level later revealed to be more than four times the legal limit.

This knowledge—that the man had made a series of poor choices culminating in his presence on that highway—should have been a balm to Hillary's conscience. But the human psyche is rarely so logical. Despite understanding on an intellectual level that she wasn't to blame, Hillary couldn't shake the horror of what had happened.

Night after night, her sleep was shattered by the same nightmare. The sickening thud of her tires rolling over the man's body. The nauseating sensation in her stomach. The terrifying question that echoed in her mind, "What was that?"

It was in our third session that I broached the idea of guided imagery. I wanted to offer Hillary hope, to show her that there were tools at our disposal that might help her put this calamity in a better place in her mind. But in my eagerness to instill confidence in my abilities (I was not yet thirty and still green), I uttered what is possibly the worst phrase I've ever used with a patient.

"Let's try this procedure, as it may help you put this trauma away forever. I'd like to think of it as just a speed bump on the road of life…" The words had barely left my mouth when I realized the horrific inappropriateness of my metaphor. "Oh my God, did I just say that?"

Thankfully, Hillary's sense of humor came to our rescue. We both burst into laughter at the sheer absurdity of my words. I quickly proclaimed it the dumbest thing I'd ever said as a licensed psychologist—a title it has held for nearly forty years since.

Despite my verbal faux pas, Hillary trusted me enough to proceed with the guided imagery. The process was relatively simple. After the requisite relaxation exercise, I guided her to a mental movie theater where she could watch the accident

one more time. I encouraged her to feel every sensation—
the thump of impact, the dread that followed, the anxiety,
vulnerability, powerlessness, and horror.

Then, I offered Hillary a choice. She could choose anyone she
wanted as a source of comfort—her higher power, a friend, a
parent, even the state trooper who had handled the accident.
Hillary, in a move that spoke volumes about her strength,
chose self-comfort. She told herself that she no longer
needed to replay this accident scene in her mind. She didn't
need an encounter with the victim; she could assume he was
free from his obvious distress, and hopefully in a better place.

The effect was almost immediate. The nightmares ceased.
The flashbacks to the highway faded. Her fear of driving and
self-recrimination dissipated. With a single session of guided
imagery, Hillary had given herself permission to let go of the
trauma and reclaim her confidence as a driver.

Nearly four decades later, Hillary is still a part of my life. She's
been in and out of therapy over the years, now grappling
with significant autoimmune illnesses and the challenges of
navigating life in a wheelchair. Through it all, she remains
an exemplary therapy patient, her quick wit and resilience
undimmed by time and trials.

Two things remain constant in our long association. First,
that single guided imagery session helped her immensely
and immediately. And second, my ill-conceived "bump in the
road" comment remains, by mutual agreement, the dumbest
thing I've ever said to her.

The power of Hillary's experience lies in its simplicity. The accident had continued to rage in her mind because it was unfinished business, laden with guilt, self-blame, and the horrible sensation of having taken a human life. The guided imagery session allowed her to give herself permission— permission to acknowledge that it wasn't her fault, that she had done the best she could in a terrible situation. The recurring "thump" in her dreams was her psyche's way of signaling the unresolved nature of the trauma. By mentally releasing her accountability for the accident and handing control back to the universe, Hillary was able to quiet that signal and reclaim her right to peace.

Gary's Golf Game: A Hole-in-One for Guided Imagery

After the weighty tales of death, trauma, combat, and life-altering accidents, it's time for a palate cleanser. Enter Gary's story—a reminder that guided imagery isn't just for processing deep-seated trauma, but can also be a powerful tool for performance enhancement.

Gary was a thirty-three-year-old big shot in a major local organization, a man with his sights set firmly on the C-suite— if not in his current company, then somewhere else in his field. He had all the ingredients for success—the education, the early career wins, what appeared to be a golden ticket to the top. But there was one thing Gary didn't have, one area where his masterful control slipped away: his golf game.

More specifically, as Gary eloquently put it, "I can't putt for shit!"

I knew Gary peripherally from local circles and was admittedly surprised when he sought my help. He struck me as one of those young titans with an ego the size of a small planet, not typically inclined to seek assistance at this stage of life. But it wasn't his marriage, career, or personality he wanted help with. It was all about his golf game, and most specifically, his poor putting.

Our initial exchange was a verbal sparring match, filled with the kind of psychology-bashing humor I knew he'd appreciate. "So, what are you hoping to accomplish by talking to a psychologist, Gary? Do you think this goes back to the breast-feeding stage of your infancy?" I quipped.

He laughed and volleyed back, "No, I thought it was more about my toilet training. I told you my putting ain't for shit."

After our banter subsided, Gary got to the point. He'd read about athletes using visualization techniques to improve their performance, and wondered if I could do something similar for his golf game.

I explained the concept of guided imagery and its applications in sports psychology. While I hadn't done extensive work in this area, I had some experience with basketball and weightlifting. I offered to try the technique with him or refer him to a sports psychologist who specialized in golf performance.

Predictably, Gary scoffed at the idea of seeing someone else. "It took a lot for me to get here because I trust you. I ain't going anywhere else. Let's make this happen."

We began with a relaxation exercise, which, to my surprise, the hard-charging Gary took to with ease. Then, I guided him to his favorite golf course in his mind's eye. I spent an inordinate amount of time ensuring Gary was fully immersed in the experience—feeling his golf shoes on the green, the breeze ruffling his hair, squinting beneath his visor at the bright sunshine, even complaining about the "effing humidity" as was his wont. I wanted the scenario to be as real as possible.

Then we focused on the putting. I had Gary examine his putter, assume his favorite stance, grip the club just so, align his eyes correctly. Then, I guided him through sinking putt after perfect putt. We started close to the hole, then moved progressively further away—one foot, three feet, seven feet, ten feet, all the way to the edge of the green. I had him visualize this scene with laser focus, blocking out all distractions.

To keep it realistic, I included some near-misses—putts that fell just short or veered slightly off course. But the overall outcome was excellent. I wanted Gary not just to see himself putting masterfully, but to feel it in his hands, his body, his very soul. This wasn't just imagination; in Gary's mind, it was happening. It was real.

The results? According to Gary, who called the following week instead of scheduling another session, his game had improved dramatically, especially his putting. He wanted me to know that the single session had made a noticeable difference.

Shortly after our session, Gary was offered his dream promotion and transferred to Minnesota. I never heard from him again, but I like to think he's out there somewhere, sinking putts with the best of them.

The key to Gary's success lies in a principle articulated by Cal Ripken Sr., father of the famous baseball "Iron Man" Cal Ripken Jr. He said, "Practice does not make perfect. Perfect practice makes perfect."[16] In other words, practicing an imperfect technique only reinforces those imperfections. What we did in our guided imagery session was allow Gary to practice perfection—to see, feel, and experience the perfect putt over and over again.

Was the improvement permanent? Without follow-up, it's impossible to say. Likely, Gary would need to continue practicing his perfect technique, both in his mind and on the green, to maintain his gains. But his experience serves as a powerful reminder of the versatility of guided imagery—a tool not just for healing trauma, but for unlocking human potential in all its forms.

Bobby's Daddy: Healing the Wounds of Abandonment

Nine-year-old "Bobby" was the kind of child that haunts elementary school teachers' nightmares. Defiant to the core, he wore his resentment like armor, lashing out at other children with an aggression that often crossed the line into physical harm. Instructions from teachers bounced off him

---

16   Pirsig, R. M. (n.d.). Robert M. Pirsig quotes. The Quotations Page. quotationspage.com/quote/31469.html

like rain off a statue, and the threat of consequences seemed to fuel rather than deter his rebellious spirit. If there was a textbook case for oppositional defiant disorder (ODD),[17] Bobby fit the bill perfectly, his behavior a symphony of defiance, sabotaging every opportunity for learning, play, or growth, be it at school or home. Conflict had become Bobby's new normal, his default mode of engaging with the world.

But as I sat with Bobby's mother during our initial intake, a different picture began to emerge. Bobby, she insisted, hadn't always been this way. The change in her son was as sudden as it was dramatic, coinciding precisely with her husband—Bobby's father—walking out on the family several months earlier. The departure had been abrupt, leaving no room for goodbyes or explanations. Bobby had neither seen nor heard from his father since that day, left to grapple with a dad-sized hole in his life without so much as a word of explanation.

In the months that followed, Bobby had sealed his lips on the subject of his father, but the chip on his shoulder spoke volumes. It was a weight that needed lifting, a wound that needed healing.

Bobby's first encounter with therapy had been less than fruitful. A young therapist had attempted a basic "reality therapy" approach, focusing on accountability for behavior and understanding consequences. Bobby, intelligent enough to play along, had given the therapist the answers he sought. But according to his mother, there had been no substantial changes in his behavior.

---

17 Vanzin, L., & Mauri, V. (2020). *Understanding Conduct Disorder and Oppositional-Defiant Disorder: A Guide to Symptoms, Management and Treatment.* Routledge.

It was a guidance counselor at Bobby's school, familiar with my work from a local speaking engagement, who suggested that a second attempt at therapy might be worthwhile. And so, Bobby found his way to my office.

In our first couple of sessions, my primary goal was to establish rapport with Bobby. We spent a significant amount of time in play—tossing a ball back and forth or engaging in ping-pong matches, activities made possible by the clinic where I worked at the time. Bobby seemed to enjoy the play and attention, particularly, I suspected, from a male adult figure. But while these interactions were positive, they weren't transformative in themselves.

It was in our third session that I proposed something different. I told Bobby I wanted to do an exercise that would help him use his imagination. His reaction was tepid at best, but he appeared compliant, which, given his rebellious streak, I took as a win.

To my pleasant surprise, Bobby followed the relaxation exercises without resistance. His breathing slowed, his restless body stilled, and he seemed to be genuinely following my instructions. After a brief relaxation induction, I encouraged Bobby to imagine meeting his father somewhere near his house, in a place where they could be alone, away from his mother and siblings.

It didn't take long for Bobby to conjure up the local park where he and his dad used to play. I asked him to imagine his father meeting him there, and then I began to speak as Bobby's father:

I'm so sorry, Bobby. I left without saying goodbye. Your mother and I can't seem to get along very well, and I needed to move away. I don't know if I'll be back again, but I want you to know that I love you and it wasn't your fault that your mom and I had problems together. I need to go away for a while, and I'm not sure where I'm going or what I'm going to do. I just don't want you to blame yourself, and please don't blame your mother either, Bobby, because she's a great lady and she loves you. Try to be good to her and do the best you can. Okay?

At this point, I asked Bobby to communicate with his father. "If you want to tell him that you're angry at him, it's okay to do that. If you are sad and you miss him, tell him that." As I mentioned the option of expressing sadness, I saw tears well up in Bobby's eyes—a telltale sign that he was deeply invested in the imagery.

I continued:

You can take a moment now and tell Dad anything you want to about what's going on in your life. But when you're finished with that, I want you to tell him goodbye and thank him for the years that you've had together. Let him know that you're gonna do the best you can with your life now, and that you'll always remember him. Let him know that you will miss him and that you will be loving and obedient to your mommy. You can say all of these things in any way you want to say them. Just please make sure that you say whatever is important for you to say.

I gave Bobby a moment to speak to the image of his father in the quiet of his mind. When he was done, signaled by the raising of his right index finger, I gently brought him back to the present, to the room with the couch in the mental health clinic.

When I asked how things went, Bobby's response was a characteristically brief, "Fine." But the real revelation came later, from his mother. "Whatever you did last time, Bobby's behavior is very different," she reported. "He is not the aggressive, impossible-to-deal-with kid that he has been since Dad left. He's more quiet, considerably less angry and explosive. I'm not sure what you did, but I like this new version of Bobby much better than the angry little boy."

Shortly after, I learned that the family had relocated, and I never saw Bobby again. But in that single session, something profound had shifted.

While we can never be entirely sure what elements of the guided imagery were most powerful and effective, two aspects stand out as potentially crucial.

First, hearing his "father" normalize his feelings, apologize for his behavior, and remove any blame from Bobby likely provided immense relief. Bobby was given permission to feel everything he felt, and those feelings were validated.

Secondly, Bobby had the chance to say goodbye to his father and let him go. Instead of holding onto his father by clinging to resentment and hurt, Bobby was able to release those feelings and, in doing so, begin to move forward.

In essence, the guided imagery provided Bobby with the closure he so desperately needed, allowing him to start healing the wounds of abandonment and rediscover his better self.

Christie's Abortion: Finding Peace in the Face of Faith

The topic of abortion is a minefield of deeply held beliefs and raw emotions. As a clinician, my role is not to sway anyone one way or the other, but to help individuals navigate their own convictions and find peace with their decisions. Over the years, I've encountered a handful of women grappling with the aftermath of abortions they found ego-dystonic—not aligned with their sense of self.

Christie was one such woman. A devout Catholic, she had made the difficult decision to terminate a pregnancy years ago, a choice that left her carrying a burden of guilt and resentment. The source of her turmoil was twofold: her deep-seated religious beliefs that viewed abortion as a grave sin, and the fact that the decision had been heavily influenced by her husband, George.

Christie and George already had six children when she found herself unexpectedly pregnant again. George, feeling overwhelmed and certain they were done expanding their family, pressured Christie to terminate the pregnancy. "A minivan is as big as I want to go," he had said. "I don't need to purchase the Partridge family's bus."

Tearfully, Christie had complied with George's wishes, not only terminating the pregnancy but also agreeing to a procedure to prevent future pregnancies. But the decision ate at her soul. As a woman who took great pride in being named after Christ, whose life goal was to raise her children according to the precepts of the church, the abortion felt like the ultimate betrayal of her faith.

For twelve years, Christie carried this burden silently, her guilt and anguish growing with each passing day. When she finally arrived at my door, she was not only grappling with her own emotions, but also harboring a deep resentment toward George.

"He might not know it," she confided, "but our sex life hasn't been anything to speak of since those procedures, and it's not all medical." The wound George's decision had inflicted ran deep, leaving Christie feeling like a "murderous mother" and a terrible person. She knew how much she loved her other children and felt certain she had room in her heart for one more.

Our first step was to bring George in for a session. Christie needed to express her feelings to him, and he needed the opportunity to understand, empathize, and validate her experience. To my relief, the session went as well as I could have hoped. George was humble and apologetic, and Christie found herself able to forgive him, drawing on her belief that they had been forgiven for all their trespasses by their Lord.

But while this session was a crucial step, it wasn't enough to heal Christie's wound completely. She still felt a significant void concerning the aborted child. It was then that I suggested we try guided imagery, offering Christie the chance to envision and experience time with this baby and, hopefully, with Jesus, in an effort to gain closure, or at least a healthier perspective.

Christie agreed, her faith making her open to the idea of a spiritual encounter, even if only in her mind's eye. We began with the usual procedure: relaxation, preparation, and then guiding Christie to a meeting with Jesus. She decided that since she had five boys and only one girl, she wanted this unborn child to be another daughter. Even saying this aloud brought tears to her eyes. We gave the little girl a name: Elizabeth.

I asked Christie to imagine a place where she could see, hear, smell, and feel the beauty of her celestial understanding of heaven. Once she indicated she had arrived in this place, I suggested that Jesus had just walked in, carrying the baby version of Elizabeth in his arms.

Only when Christie could see Jesus's loving face holding her precious image of Elizabeth did we continue. With tears streaming down her face, I began to speak as Jesus:

> I am so pleased that you were able to come and see us, Christie. I know that seeing your baby for the first time means so much to you. I want you to know that Elizabeth is not terminated, she is alive and well and with me. She is loved. She is well taken care of. She is precious and beautiful and will have a life in the great beyond that you cannot comprehend while on Earth.

She is a joy to me, and she is very much my child, even as you are. I want you to know that you will be reunited with her one day, as it says in the twenty-third Psalm that I know you know—you will both "dwell in the house of the Lord forever."

Continuing in the voice of Jesus, I asked, "Would you like to hold Elizabeth?"

Christie nodded tearfully, her arms reaching out. In a spontaneous decision, I placed a stuffed bear in her arms for her to hold, allowing her to physically enact the embrace she was experiencing in her mind. For several minutes, Christie held and rocked the bear, her tears flowing freely. After about five minutes, I gently asked if she was ready to give Elizabeth back to Jesus, with the promise that she was alive, well, and would be there for Christie when her time on Earth was through.

To my relief and joy, Christie allowed me to take the stuffed bear from her hands. Within minutes, I guided her back to the present moment in my office. The change in Christie was palpable—she seemed lighter, as if a great weight had been lifted from her shoulders.

According to Christie, this guided imagery session was exactly what she needed. Three crucial elements combined to bring her a sense of profound relief:

1. Christie felt forgiven by her Lord, alleviating the guilt of what she had perceived as an unpardonable sin.

2. She realized that her daughter was not destroyed, but rather promoted to another level, where she was thriving.

3. Christie was assured that she would be reunited with Elizabeth one day when her own earthly life was over.

These realizations transformed Christie's perspective entirely. The very fabric of her depression—the perception of hopelessness—had been rewoven into a tapestry of hope, peace, and anticipation of a joyful reunion.

Christie continued therapy with me for a while longer, working to resolve other aspects of her life and further strengthen her relationship with George. But when it came to the abortion, she was at peace. Her guided imagery experience had allowed her to reconcile her faith, her actions, and her hope for the future, freeing her from the burden she had carried for so long.

In both Bobby's and Christie's cases, guided imagery provided a bridge between reality and the spiritual or emotional needs of the individual. It offered a safe space to confront painful truths, express suppressed emotions, and find a path to healing that aligned with their personal beliefs and values. These stories serve as powerful reminders of the technique's versatility and its potential to bring peace and closure even in the most complex and sensitive situations.

Jane and the Unrelenting Defibrillator: Taming the Storm Within

I loved working with Jane. Her presence in my waiting room never failed to bring a smile to my face. A vibrant woman in her mid-fifties, "divorced and not looking," Jane was a force of nature—loud at times, irreverent always, but unfailingly funny. Her sarcastic wit offered a fresh and entertaining perspective on just about anything life threw her way.

We had made some early progress in treating her anxiety and helping her cope with various medical issues. But one day, Jane brought in a new challenge that overshadowed all her previous concerns, a problem that had come to dominate every aspect of her life.

Jane was morbidly obese and grappling with significant cardiac issues. As a result, her cardiologist had inserted a defibrillator—a device designed to shock her heart back into rhythm if she were in danger of succumbing to a heart attack. For about a year, Jane's body seemed to have accommodated the defibrillator without incident. Then, one day, all hell broke loose.

From the few patients I've treated with defibrillators, I've learned that no one enjoys the experience of the device firing. It's always a shock (no pun intended), often catching individuals off guard and sometimes even knocking them to the ground. But Jane's experience went beyond the typical.

It happened one day as she sat at home, in front of her TV. The defibrillator fired, shocking Jane into screaming an expletive as she realized what had occurred. Seated comfortably in her chair, she tried to reassure herself, "This is okay, I got this."

But things were far from fine. The defibrillator fired a second time. And a third. And then several more times until Jane realized this was not normal—it wasn't about saving her life anymore. Something had malfunctioned. She called 911 and was told, in no uncertain terms, to "Get your ass to the emergency room! Now!"

Fortunately, Jane wasn't alone. Her friend rushed her to the hospital, doing her "best rendition of 'Fast and Fucking Furious' all the way to the ER."

Although Jane was fortunate enough to bypass the typical seven-hour emergency room wait, the ER staff had never seen anything like her experience. Reduced to tears, Jane begged one nurse to unplug the device. When told doing so would kill her, she could only respond, "I know."

"It would not stop firing," Jane recounted, her voice still trembling at the memory. "Every time it did, I would scream another F-bomb, until the ER had more bombs than a war zone. Can you imagine what that was like, Dr. Cortman, having that effing thing go off 103 times? Yes, I counted. Let me tell you in the best way I know how: Do you remember in those Roadrunner cartoons when Wile E. Coyote swallows a stick of dynamite and blows up from the inside out? That's what it felt like, but not once and not twice, but 103 times!"

There are times when the best a psychologist can do is shake their head and empathize. "Oh my God, that sounds horrible!"

I exclaimed. "I am so sorry! I can't even imagine what that would be like... Wow!" Then, unable to resist lightening the mood, I added, "But you're not being fair to me, because I keep seeing Wile E. Coyote's eyeballs bugging out of his head when the dynamite explodes, and I just need a minute to laugh at that image."

We both burst into laughter, expelling nervous energy and reconnecting after her harrowing tale. I wanted to shift the intensity of the mood and send a reassuring message that it was over and she would be okay. From her research since the incident, Jane had learned that her experience was unprecedented. As far as she knew, she held the world record for defibrillator misfires. This became part of her sarcastic repertoire, her trump card to top anyone else's "shit story."

But Jane wasn't in my office just to entertain me with her crazy experience. She wanted to feel "normal again." I was determined to help her move past this absurd and traumatic event as quickly as possible.

We began with a cognitive-behavioral therapy (CBT) approach, challenging her to replace catastrophic thinking about the relentless defibrillator with a mindset of relief and gratitude. We focused on celebrating her survivorship and resilience.

While this approach was helpful, it wasn't curative. Jane remained tethered to her chair in front of the TV, not because of any medical instruction to live a sedentary life, but out of fear. She was afraid to move, to exert herself, to live. Ironically, that chair—associated with the onset of the psychotic defibrillator—had become both her prison and her sanctuary. If worst came to worst, she knew she could survive again in that chair. Everywhere else on earth was suspect in Jane's post-trauma logic.

It was time to introduce guided imagery. Jane was somewhat desperate, but also quite comfortable in her inertia. She was safe in her chair and didn't really need to do anything else in her life, as she was disabled and not currently engaged in a routine that required her to leave the confines of her living room. Still, Jane knew that she needed to get out of that chair, with which she now had a love-hate relationship.

As we processed the idea of guided imagery together, I emphasized that our goal was to help her feel, experience, and release whatever she was holding onto from that experience that kept her stuck, both mentally and physically. We began with the relaxation component, and Jane complied, her breathing rate significantly reducing as she settled into the La-Z-Boy chair in my office.

Instead of using the movie theater scenario, I wanted Jane to revisit the entire experience, from the onset of the defibrillator's first discharge to the ride to the ER and through the hospital experience. Jane requested to talk to me throughout the procedure, processing her feelings as the situation unfolded. It was as if she was going through it again, but this time narrating her process, with an emphasis on her thoughts and feelings.

As you can imagine, it wasn't just about physical pain and shock. Jane expressed feelings of powerlessness and helplessness, fear of total loss of control, the hopelessness of feeling that it would never stop, and the willingness to do anything to make it stop, including unplugging the device and facing death. I challenged her to feel all of this in the moment and then make a decision that she no longer needed to keep these feelings, having worked through them.

I asked Jane to release the hypervigilance—the need to remain on guard 24/7—to ensure this couldn't happen again. I encouraged her to let go of the fear, reminding her that she had already faced the worst thing that could ever happen with this device and had essentially won the battle. I asked her to imagine letting go of these feelings because she didn't need them anymore. In their place, I urged her to embrace a sense of well-being and pride that she had gone through something so horrific and emerged victorious.

Finally, I asked Jane to speak to herself confidently, acknowledging that it was time to get involved again with her friends and activities—to return to the life she had known before the incident.

As is often the case in my experience, the procedure left Jane feeling drained. She emerged relaxed and peaceful, but depleted. I wouldn't know anything more about the success of the guided imagery technique that day.

But over the next couple of weeks, I learned that Jane was getting out of the house again. She even attended a party thrown by her best friend—a gathering, she discovered, that was held in her honor, celebrating her ongoing recovery from the incident.

Jane's sister had been paying for her therapy sessions, as Jane wasn't working and couldn't afford them on her own. Once the guided imagery allowed her to gradually return to her life, we discontinued treatment. And because this isn't a Hollywood story with a perfectly tied bow at the end, I haven't spoken to Jane in probably five or six years. But I do know that she was functioning again and, according to a card she sent me, was deeply grateful for the success of the procedure and the wonderful connection of our therapeutic relationship.

Jane's story serves as a powerful reminder of the mind-body connection and the potential of guided imagery to bridge the gap between physical trauma and psychological healing. By revisiting her harrowing experience in a controlled, supportive environment, Jane was able to process her fears, reclaim her sense of control, and ultimately, step back into her life.

Conclusion: The Transformative Power of Guided Imagery

As we've journeyed through these diverse stories—from Kerri's surfing accident to Doug's lifelong anxiety, from Hillary's tragic car accident to Gary's golf game, from Bobby's abandonment issues to Christie's spiritual crisis, and finally to Jane's medical trauma—we've witnessed the remarkable versatility and power of guided imagery.

This technique, seemingly simple in its execution, has demonstrated an uncanny ability to address a wide array of human experiences and challenges:

1. **Trauma Resolution:** For Kerri, Hillary, and Jane, guided imagery provided a safe space to revisit and reprocess traumatic events, allowing them to integrate these experiences into their life stories without being perpetually haunted by them.

2. **Anxiety Reduction:** Doug's story showcases how guided imagery can sometimes produce dramatic and lasting effects on chronic anxiety, even when the root cause stretches back decades.

3. **Performance Enhancement:** Gary's improved golf game illustrates how guided imagery can be used to enhance skills and performance, not just in sports, but potentially in any area of life requiring mental focus and physical execution.

4. **Emotional Healing:** Bobby's story demonstrates how guided imagery can provide closure and emotional healing, particularly in cases of abandonment or unresolved relationship issues.

5. **Spiritual Reconciliation:** Christie's experience highlights the potential of guided imagery to bridge the gap between actions and deeply held beliefs, offering a path to peace even in the face of profound spiritual conflict.

6. **Physical and Psychological Recovery:** Jane's case underscores the power of guided imagery in addressing the psychological aftermath of physical trauma, illustrating the deep connection between mind and body in the healing process.

Throughout these stories, several key themes emerge:

- **The Power of the Mind:** Time and again, we've seen how the mind's ability to create vivid, emotionally resonant experiences can lead to real-world changes in behavior, emotion, and even physical performance.

- **Safety and Control:** Guided imagery provides a safe environment for individuals to confront fears, process trauma, and practice new behaviors or thought patterns. The sense of control this offers can be profoundly empowering.

- **Personalization:** The effectiveness of guided imagery often lies in its ability to be tailored to each individual's unique experiences, beliefs, and needs. Whether it's meeting a departed loved one or visualizing the perfect golf swing, the imagery is deeply personal and thus deeply impactful.

- **Integration of Past and Present:** Many of these stories involve bringing past experiences into the present moment for reprocessing and integration, allowing individuals to move forward without being tethered to past traumas or limiting beliefs.

- **Immediate and Lasting Impact:** While not universally true, many of these cases show both immediate and long-lasting effects from even a single session of guided imagery, challenging our assumptions about the pace of psychological change.

As mental health professionals, these stories remind us of the incredible potential lying dormant in the human mind. Guided imagery offers us a tool to tap into this potential, to help our clients rewrite their internal narratives, confront their deepest fears, and unlock new possibilities for growth and healing.

However, it's crucial to remember that guided imagery is not a one-size-fits-all solution. Its effectiveness can vary based on the individual, the specific issue at hand, and the skill of the practitioner. It's often most powerful when used as part of a comprehensive therapeutic approach, tailored to the unique needs of each client.

As we continue to explore and refine this technique, we open doors to new possibilities in psychological healing and personal growth. The stories in this chapter are not just testimonials to the power of guided imagery; they are invitations to all of us—practitioners and patients alike—to harness the remarkable capacity of the human mind to transform our lives, one image at a time.

Chapter Nine
Guided Imagery and Sports: Visualizing Victory

The Genesis of Mental Training in Athletics

The marriage of mind and muscle in sports performance isn't a recent phenomenon. As early as the 1960s, tennis legend Billie Jean King was reportedly harnessing the power of visualization to elevate her game. Concurrently, Al Oerter, the four-time Olympic discus champion, was employing similar mental techniques to great effect.

Since these pioneering days, the practice of simulating competitive sports performance through imagery has evolved into a sophisticated and multifaceted discipline. Modern sports psychologists emphasize the importance of creating a holistic mental experience. As Nicole Dettling, a renowned sports psychologist, aptly puts it, "The more the athlete can imagine the entire package, the better it's going to be."

This evolution has led to a semantic shift from "visualization" to "imagery," reflecting a more comprehensive sensory approach. American aerial skier Emily Cook explains, "You have to smell it. You have to hear it. You have to feel it, everything." This multisensory approach creates a more immersive and effective mental rehearsal.

Olympic-Level Mental Preparation

The 2014 Winter Olympics marked a watershed moment for sports psychology, with no fewer than nine sports psychologists serving the US Olympic team. These experts helped athletes engage in various psychological techniques, including guided imagery, to refine their performance. Olympians learned to imagine their events in exquisite detail, from "point A to point Z," envisioning everything from the chairlift ride up the mountain to the wind on their necks and the roar of the crowd.

This comprehensive imagery served dual purposes: perfecting technique and managing pre-competition anxiety. As Cook attests, "I don't think I could possibly do a jump, or especially a new trick without having this imagery process... For me, this is so very key to the athlete I've become."

Beyond the Olympics: The Broad Impact of Guided Imagery

The application of guided imagery extends far beyond elite-level competitions. A fascinating study I once encountered illustrates this point perfectly. The research examined three groups of sixth-grade students and their basketball free-throw efficiency:

1. A control group that didn't practice at all

2. A group that practiced shooting daily for six weeks

3. A group that only practiced via imagery for six weeks

The results were astounding. While the control group showed no improvement, the physical practice group improved by 23 percent. Remarkably, the imagery-only group improved by 22 percent—nearly matching the performance of those who practiced physically.[18] This study sparked my imagination, making me ponder all the life tasks I'd prefer to accomplish through mental rehearsal alone!

The Power of Mental Practice

Subsequent research has continued to demonstrate the potency of guided imagery in sports:

- Basketball players using mental imagery showed significant improvements in vertical jump

---

18   Breakthrough Basketball. (n.d.). Basketball visualization techniques to improve your game. breakthroughbasketball.com/mental/visualization.html

performance over those who didn't (Shahbazi &
Tahmasebi, 2007).

- Football players who combined guided imagery with
specific verbal cues demonstrated improved field
goal kicking accuracy over those who only practiced
physically (Post, Wrisberg & Mullins, 2012).

Consider the implications of these findings. In the NFL, where
approximately 20 percent[19] of games are decided by three
points or less (the margin of a single field goal), having a
kicker who utilizes both physical and mental practice could
provide a decisive advantage.

Broader Benefits of Guided Imagery in Sports

The positive impact of guided imagery extends beyond
physical performance:

- Imagery about exercise has been shown to foster more
positive attitudes toward physical activity, potentially
enhancing exercise adherence and motivation.[20]
- When combined with physical practice, imagery led to
greater improvements in strength performance than
physical practice alone.[21]

19 Sports Insights. (2022, July 25). Examining NFL key numbers for over/unders. sportsinsights.com/
blog/examining-nfl-key-numbers-overunders

20 Markland, D., Hall, C. R., Duncan, L. R., & Simatovic, J. (2015). The effects of an imagery intervention
on implicit and explicit exercise attitudes. Psychology of Sport and Exercise, 17, 24–31.

21 Wright, C. J., & Smith, D. (2016). The effects of PETTLEP imagery on strength performance.
International Journal of Sport and Exercise Psychology, 14(3), 269–280.

- Swimmers utilizing guided imagery demonstrated significant improvements in race times over a control group.[22]

- Multiple studies have shown guided imagery to be effective in reducing performance anxiety and improving overall athletic performance.[23]

Conclusion

While this overview is far from exhaustive, the collective research paints a compelling picture of guided imagery's positive impact on various aspects of sports performance. From skill acquisition and improvement to anxiety reduction, motivation enhancement, and sport-specific skill refinement, guided imagery has proven its worth across a spectrum of athletic disciplines. I am not a sports psychologist, but I am a sports junkie.

As we continue to unravel the intricate connections between mind and body, guided imagery stands as a powerful tool in an athlete's mental arsenal. Whether you're a weekend warrior or an Olympic hopeful, incorporating this technique into your training regimen could be the key to unlocking your full athletic potential. After all, in the world of sports, the battle is often won in the mind before it ever begins on the field.

22 Woolfolk, R. L., Parrish, M. W., & Murphy, S. M. (1993). Effects of imagery training on swimming performance: An applied study. *Imagination, Cognition and Personality*, 13(2), 153–166.

23 Hale, B. D., & Whitehouse, A. (2002). The effect of guided imagery practice on competitive anxiety in young elite athletes. *Journal of Applied Sport Psychology*, 14(2), 149–161.

Chapter Ten

How to Conduct a Guided Imagery Session

Here's a startling yet valid statement about guided imagery: it often produces more healing and closure in a single session than a traumatized individual has managed to achieve on their own over decades.

The Power of Guided Imagery

Guided imagery, as the term suggests, requires a facilitator—ideally an experienced therapist, not your hairdresser—to guide you through the experience. Your role is to follow the suggestions, creating in your mind a scenario as immersive as reality itself. If you were to engage in a guided imagery session with me, here's what you might experience:

1. Relaxation Techniques

The journey begins with relaxation. The goal is to have your entire body unwind from head to toe, using two primary techniques:

1. **Progressive Muscle Relaxation:** This involves tensing each muscle group for five seconds, then releasing. Once flexed, each muscle group returns to a lower state of resting tension.

2. **Deep Breathing:** Inhale to a count of three, hold your breath for a few seconds, then exhale to a count of five. This altered ratio of oxygen to carbon dioxide in the blood stimulates an additional relaxation response.

2. Comfortable Positioning

Find a comfortable position, seated or reclined, and close your eyes. Focus on your breathing, this time allowing it to occur naturally. If I observe signs of tension—fidgeting, frowning, or discomfort—I might employ additional visualization techniques:

1. **Staircase Descent:** Imagine descending a flight of stairs, with each step representing a deeper state of relaxation.

2. **Tranquilizer Visualization:** Picture being injected with a powerful tranquilizer, visualized as a sky-blue substance moving through your body. As it travels, the blue color replaces a hot neon crimson that represents stress, tension, pain, trauma, or anything requiring release.

3. The Theater of the Mind

Once fully relaxed, I'll guide you to imagine a door. Behind it lies a movie theater where you'll watch a significant scene unfold on the big screen. You're given a remote control, symbolizing your power over the experience—you can play, pause, fast-forward, rewind, and stop at will.

4. Confronting the Past

You'll watch the entire "movie" from beginning to end. Afterward, I'll invite you, at your current age, to enter the scene and provide comfort and solace to the younger version of yourself who's suffering. This might involve asking an abuser to leave or offering comfort to your younger self. You may ask for further support by imagining your life partner, therapist, higher power, etc., joining you!

5. Symbolism and Closure

After processing a traumatic scene, I might have you imagine a projectionist offering you a DVD of the movie. You can take this "DVD" outside and destroy it, symbolizing that the event is over and no longer has power over you.

6. Grief Work and Unfinished Business

For grief-related issues, the imagery might involve opening a door into a meaningful location—a living room, a favorite cabin in the woods, or a childhood kitchen. Here, we create a conversation between you and the person you're grieving. This could be someone lost in an accident, an estranged child who died without reconciliation, a spouse who died suddenly, or anyone with whom you have unfinished business.

In these scenarios, I speak for the deceased individual to facilitate closure. This often involves:

- Apologies for past hurts or betrayals
- Expressions of love that were difficult to communicate in life
- Allowing you to express hurt, anger, or rage toward someone who mistreated or abandoned you
- Acknowledgement from the perpetrator of a trauma
- Expressing appreciation and gratitude that wasn't fully conveyed while the person was alive

Why Does Guided Imagery Work?

All human relationships are naturally unfinished works in progress. Parents are expected to nurture; children are expected to grow up. When a relationship completes its natural cycle, expectations are satisfied. A good son transitions from being a good man to being a good father.

Traumatic events, however, interrupt this natural flow of life events and produce experiences of loss. These events are often consciously or unconsciously avoided and sealed off from conscious experience. Their treatment, therefore, involves two key steps:

1. Making the traumatic event accessible to conscious awareness through guided imagery.

2. Modifying the context or adding elements that complete the relationship or resolve the trauma, thus helping move it to a better place in one's psyche.

What's experienced in imagery is processed as reality by the nervous system and feels genuinely real to the individual. This is why guided imagery can be so powerful—it allows for the reprocessing of traumatic memories in a safe, controlled environment, facilitating healing and closure that might otherwise take years to achieve.

What Happens After a Successful Session?

So, your guided imagery session was a remarkable success. Perhaps you were finally able to say goodbye to a departed sibling, find peace after childhood abuse, or achieve closure regarding the loss of a child. Does this mean therapy is complete?

Like many questions in psychology, the answer isn't straightforward: it depends on your individual circumstances and needs.

Some clients, having found the peace and closure they sought, choose to end treatment. Many tell me they'll call if they need further support, but their presenting issue has been resolved. Recall Todd's story from Chapter One—after successfully processing the trauma of the cycling accident through guided imagery, he didn't require further sessions.

Others continue therapy long after a successful guided imagery experience, as they have multiple issues to address. Take Beth's case from Chapter Four. While guided imagery helped her process her sexual assault in a single session, our therapeutic relationship has spanned years, addressing various traumas and helping her overcome alcohol addiction. She still visits on an as-needed basis, recognizing that life's challenges sometimes require professional support to process and navigate effectively.

Some clients maintain therapy throughout their adult lives, managing long-standing issues with depression, anxiety, personality disorders, or addictions. While resolving a specific trauma through guided imagery can be transformative, it doesn't necessarily address all aspects of one's mental health challenges.

Consider a client with a fear of drowning. Guided imagery might help them process the traumatic event that sparked this fear, but they still need to learn to swim. Similarly, using guided imagery to heal from childhood abuse can be profoundly helpful, but it won't automatically resolve relationship difficulties or anger management issues that may have developed as a result of that trauma.

In cases of dissociative identity disorder, my extensive experience has shown that treatment typically requires addressing multiple traumatic incidents, allowing each alter personality to process their experiences and integrate them into the host personality's consciousness. This process often necessitates multiple guided imagery sessions combined with other therapeutic approaches.

The decision to continue therapy after a successful guided imagery session should be based on several factors:

- The presence of other unresolved issues
- Ongoing mental health challenges
- The need for additional coping skills or strategies
- The desire for continued support in personal growth

As a clinician, I make recommendations about continuing therapy based on my assessment of these factors. While most patients trust these suggestions, especially after experiencing success with guided imagery, the final decision always rests with them. I remind my patients that they are, in effect, my employers—they have the power to continue or terminate our therapeutic relationship as they see fit.

The key is to recognize that while guided imagery can be a powerful tool for healing specific traumas or resolving particular issues, it may be just one component of a broader journey toward mental health and personal growth. Whether that journey requires additional sessions or concludes with a successful guided imagery experience depends entirely on your individual needs and circumstances.

Chapter Eleven

Pitfalls and Contraindications to Guided Imagery

I n the realm of therapeutic techniques, guided imagery stands as a beacon of hope, often yielding transformative results. Yet, like any powerful tool, it comes with its own set of challenges and potential pitfalls. As a practitioner with four decades of experience, I've witnessed the profound impact of this method—both its triumphs and its occasional shortcomings.

Recently, a serendipitous discovery allowed me to review every guided imagery session I've facilitated since adopting my current software. This treasure trove of data, spanning sessions with patients I hadn't seen in fifteen, twenty, or more years, revealed an overwhelming trend: the vast majority of outcomes were nothing short of remarkable, frequently described as "life-changing" or "miraculous."

However, even with a success rate surpassing 90 percent, there were instances where the good Dr. Cortman, as it were, laid an egg. In this chapter, we'll dissect these outliers, focusing on what went awry—or at least, what failed to work—and why. Through this exploration, we aim to enhance our understanding and application of guided imagery.

Four Primary Categories of Pitfalls

1. Inability to experience the imagery as real

2. Unwillingness to relinquish emotional attachments

3. Misrepresentation of key figures in the imagery

4. Interference from psychotic or fragile mental states

1. The Reality Gap: When Imagery Fails to Materialize

Over the years, I've encountered a handful of individuals who seemed impervious to the relaxation necessary for effective guided imagery. While resistance likely plays a role in some cases, it's crucial to acknowledge that visualization abilities vary widely among individuals.

A recent patient's reflection on experiencing pain while bidding farewell to his wife of half a century illuminates this challenge:

> Hi Doc, I reviewed my notes on the imagery session, and interestingly, there was no mention of visual imagery

or pain during it...although it was quite painful to me. I wonder if there's a correlation between pain and effectiveness. Nonetheless, it helped tremendously.

Given that patients often sidestep difficult topics in therapy—skipping homework, missing sessions, avoiding crucial conversations—it's unsurprising that some might use an "inability to connect" with guided imagery as a form of avoidance. Some have even candidly admitted to this.

However, it's imperative to recognize that some individuals genuinely struggle with visualization. As someone who doesn't visualize particularly well myself (a trait that has served me well when hearing gruesome accounts of abuse), I understand that some people are naturally more inclined to excel at this procedure than others.

Recommendation: Assess a person's visualization skills before the procedure. Have them close their eyes and conjure a specific image, such as a purple polka-dotted rhinoceros frolicking on a beach, to gauge their ability.

It's also worth evaluating a patient's capacity to relax, although I've found that even highly anxious individuals can often achieve relaxation with guided instruction. Relaxation skills can be honed with practice, and some patients may need to work on this as homework before they're prepared for guided imagery.

I cannot overemphasize this point: When the imagery is experienced as "so real," the procedure works almost without fail. In fact, I can't recall a single instance where a patient found the experience genuinely real and we didn't achieve extraordinary results.

2. The Tenacious Grip: When Letting Go Proves Challenging

The second category of obstacles involves patients who aren't prepared to release something I'm challenging them to let go. Three cases stand out:

First, a patient involved in a motorcycle accident was grappling with typical PTSD symptoms: daily flashbacks to the accident and distress over his injured leg and totaled bike. The imagery didn't seem to alleviate these symptoms— at least not until his attorney settled with the insurance company out of court several weeks later. In retrospect, it's clear that he needed to hold onto his symptoms to maintain his legal case. Letting go prematurely could have undermined his claim that the accident had significant lasting effects.

A similar situation involved a woman whose relative fell victim to a mass shooting. The imagery failed to help her bid farewell to her sister, likely because she was embroiled in an ongoing lawsuit that made it impractical to release the horror of her loss before achieving the desired legal outcome. (See Chapter Thirteen.)

Lastly, I worked with a woman who lost her husband to homicide. Witnessing her intense anguish compelled me to attempt to mitigate her pain by facilitating a goodbye to him, allowing for an exchange of love and gratitude. In hindsight, it was premature. The wound was too raw, and she wasn't ready to accept his sudden, senseless death. She required more time and ongoing treatment to let him go gradually. While she ultimately made significant progress in treatment, it wasn't necessarily due to the "magic" of guided imagery.

3. The Miscast Role: When Characters Ring False

I'll be candid: I've shouldered some incredible responsibilities when speaking for people I've never met during imagery sessions. How can one possibly channel the words of a patient's late grandfather, drug-addicted son, assailant, or even a divine figure?

As I reflect on this, I'm tempted to commend myself, given the countless patients who have remarked, "Doc, you captured it perfectly. That's exactly what my wife would have said," or "It never felt like you speaking; it was as if my mother was addressing me directly."

However, there was one notable misstep: a challenging patient with a history of depression, negativity, and self-deprecation attributed much of her struggles to her critical, abusive father. I attempted to facilitate healing by having her confront him and receive an acknowledgement of her pain and an apology from beyond the grave. I didn't progress far before she opened her eyes and interjected, "This isn't real. My dad would never apologize for anything."

The lesson was clear. She wasn't prepared to relinquish her resentment toward her father or abandon the familiar narrative that she was unloved, unlovable, and destined to underachieve, just as her father had predicted.

Or perhaps I had overstepped by scripting an apology for him.

This experience underscores the importance of gauging how much a person truly desires change versus how vital it is for them to cling to the cornerstone of their distress.

4. The Fragile Mind: When Reality Blurs

Early in my career, a patient recovering from paranoid schizophrenia imparted a valuable lesson. When I proposed guided imagery, he gently rebuked me, saying, "I've experienced seeing things that weren't real. I need to remain grounded in reality from now on." His insight was profound, and provided an important learning experience for a young clinician.

More recently, I worked with a young man grappling with PTSD and psychotic episodes, stemming from the loss of his twin brother by drowning. I attempted to help him make peace with this loss through guided imagery, envisioning a serene reunion in the afterlife. However, I later learned that his imagery included his brother being dragged to hell by demons—a manifestation of his ongoing psychotic issues that I couldn't have anticipated.

Despite this unsettling experience, this patient remains under my care and is making gradual but significant progress, primarily through using CBT principles to challenge and correct distorted thinking patterns.

Legal Consideration: If I were an attorney perusing this book, I'd advise having patients sign a waiver protecting the clinician from any unforeseen mental experiences during or after an imagery session. This is a prudent step I recommend to all practitioners employing this technique.

Conclusion

While these four potential pitfalls warrant careful consideration before engaging in guided imagery, I steadfastly maintain that the potential for healing and closure far outweighs the risks to the patient. This conviction is born from four decades of successfully wielding this powerful therapeutic tool.

As we navigate the complex landscape of the human psyche, guided imagery remains a beacon of hope and transformation. By acknowledging and preparing for these potential challenges, we can harness its power more effectively, bringing light to the darkest corners of our patients' minds and hearts.

Chapter Twelve

Future Implications and Concluding Thoughts: The Untapped Potential of Guided Imagery

In the twilight of the twentieth century, a colleague introduced me to a novel approach for treating PTSD—a technique that seemed, at first blush, more akin to parlor tricks than serious psychotherapy. This method, which involved patients moving their eyes rhythmically while recalling traumatic experiences, struck us both as superfluous, if not outright absurd. After all, we had achieved considerable success with our existing trauma treatment protocols. How could such a seemingly simplistic intervention hope to compete?

Little did we anticipate that this technique, known as eye movement desensitization and reprocessing (EMDR), would soon revolutionize the landscape of trauma therapy. Like a virulent strain of intellectual kudzu, EMDR workshops proliferated across the professional development landscape. Before long, no respectable therapy practice could claim completeness without at least one EMDR-certified practitioner on staff. Prestigious publications, from the hallowed pages of the Harvard Mental Health Letter to specialized trauma journals, sang paeans to Francine Shapiro's groundbreaking approach.

In the intervening years, EMDR has ascended to the pantheon of evidence-based trauma treatments, widely regarded as the gold standard in the field. Its pervasiveness in mental health circles has spawned a phenomenon reminiscent of pharmaceutical advertising: patients now actively seek out the technique, approaching their therapists with the same certainty one might exhibit when ordering a well-known brand. One can almost envision a dystopian future where fast-food drive-throughs offer EMDR sessions alongside their value meals: "Would you like some eye movements with those fries?"

The meteoric rise of EMDR raises the question: how did this particular therapeutic approach achieve such dominance? While a definitive answer eludes us, one cannot help but marvel at the technique's apparent marketability—a strategy seemingly culled from the playbooks of such iconic brands as Coca-Cola, Amazon, or the NFL.

However, let me be clear: this book is not intended as a jealous screed against EMDR's overwhelming success. Rather, it serves as a clarion call, heralding the arrival of an equally potent, yet woefully underutilized, technique for addressing trauma, grief, and a host of other psychological maladies. In my not-so-humble opinion (NSHO), guided imagery stands as the most efficacious approach available, though its recognition largely remains confined to the realms of relaxation and pain management.

This tome will have fulfilled its purpose if it catalyzes a wave of research initiatives across universities, government agencies, clinics, and hospitals—studies that incorporate guided imagery as elucidated within these pages. Such investigations should explore its efficacy in treating both acute and chronic trauma, unresolved grief, anxiety disorders, sleep disturbances, and phobias. Moreover, the potential applications of guided imagery extend far beyond the clinical setting, offering promising avenues for enhancing sports performance, academic achievement, and public speaking prowess.

Envision a world where individuals truly embrace the notion that success, first visualized in the mind's eye, can manifest in tangible reality. From steeling oneself for a challenging conversation with a superior to mustering the courage to pursue romantic interests, from achieving athletic milestones to conquering the fear of public speaking—guided imagery could serve as the skeleton key, unlocking human potential across myriad domains.

I posit, with unwavering conviction, that guided imagery deserves a place of prominence in every undergraduate and graduate program in psychiatry, psychology, social work, and related therapeutic disciplines. Primary care physicians and family practitioners should be well-versed in its applications, recognizing that many patients grappling with depression, anxiety, or addictive behaviors could benefit immensely from this powerful technique. It offers a proactive approach to addressing unresolved traumas and unfinished emotional business, providing an alternative to the often ineffective "time heals all wounds" philosophy.

Recent research has drawn compelling parallels between trauma and addiction, likening their relationship to that of smoking and cancer.[24] In light of these findings, it is imperative that we equip healthcare providers with tools like guided imagery to help patients process and release traumatic experiences, rather than relying on the passive and often futile approach of waiting for time to work its dubious magic.

Few endeavors would bring me greater professional satisfaction than spearheading a movement to popularize this underutilized yet highly effective technique in the mental health arena. In the interim, I remain steadfastly committed to refining, expanding, and promoting the effectiveness, versatility, and visibility of guided imagery.

So, the next time you find yourself in pursuit of continuing medical education credits and a clinical technique that promises to revolutionize your practice, I implore you to consider delving into the transformative world of guided imagery. You may well discover it to be the paradigm-shifting tool you've long sought to elevate your therapeutic arsenal.

---

24 Cortman, C., & Walden, J. (2018). *Keep Pain in the Past: Getting Over Trauma, Grief,* and the *Worst That's Ever Happened to You.* Books That Save Lives.

Three Challenges for the Future of Guided Imagery

As we look to the future of guided imagery in mental health, several challenges must be addressed:

1. Standardization and Quality Control

As guided imagery gains popularity, there's a risk of dilution and misapplication. The field must establish standardized training protocols and certification processes to ensure practitioners are adequately prepared to use this powerful technique effectively and ethically.

2. Integration with Emerging Technologies

With the rapid advancement of virtual and augmented reality technologies, there's an opportunity to enhance guided imagery experiences. However, this integration must be done thoughtfully, ensuring that the core therapeutic benefits are not lost in the pursuit of technological novelty.

3. Overcoming Skepticism and Misconceptions

Despite its potential, guided imagery may face resistance from both practitioners and patients who view it as "new age" or lacking scientific rigor.

Overcoming these perceptions will require robust research, effective communication of results, and education efforts targeted at both the professional community and the general public.

By addressing these challenges head-on, we can pave the way for guided imagery to take its rightful place as a cornerstone of modern mental health treatment.

As we look to the future of guided imagery, it's crucial to reflect on what we've learned throughout this book. The following considerations summarize the power and versatility of this technique, reinforcing its potential as a transformative tool in mental health treatment.

Final Considerations: The Multifaceted Power of Guided Imagery

As we conclude our exploration of guided imagery, let's reflect on the key insights that emerge from the wealth of experiences and research presented in this book:

Versatility

Guided imagery stands out as a remarkably adaptable technique. Its applications span a wide spectrum of human experiences and challenges, from overcoming grief and resolving trauma to reducing anxiety, gaining closure on unfinished business, and even enhancing performance in sports, music, and the arts. The potential applications extend far beyond what we've covered here, hinting at a vast, untapped potential in various domains of human behavior and well-being.

Rapid Results

One of the most striking aspects of guided imagery is its capacity for swift intervention. The majority of case studies presented in this book demonstrate significant progress achieved in just a single session. This efficiency sets guided imagery apart in a field where long-term interventions are often the norm.

Long-Lasting Effects

Perhaps even more impressive than the speed of results is their durability. Our case studies consistently reveal that successful guided imagery sessions often lead to permanent or long-term resolution of issues. This persistence of positive outcomes underscores the profound impact of the technique on the human psyche.

Multisensory Engagement

The most impactful guided imagery sessions invariably involve vivid, multisensory experiences that feel undeniably real to the patient. Indicators of deep engagement include emotional responses such as tears, rapid eye movements, and patients' post-session assertions of the experience's visceral reality. This immersive quality is key to the technique's effectiveness.

Spiritual Integration

Many patients find it natural and beneficial to incorporate their spiritual or religious beliefs into the imagery process. This integration often enhances the power and personal relevance of the experience, allowing for deeper healing and insight.

Safety and Control

Guided imagery provides a unique opportunity for patients to confront their most disturbing and frightening experiences in a safe, controlled environment. The presence of a trained professional ensures that patients can navigate these challenging mental landscapes with support and guidance.

Closure and Resolution

One of the most potent aspects of guided imagery is its ability to facilitate closure on long-standing "unfinished business." Many patients find resolution to issues that have plagued them for years, if not decades.

Limitations

It's important to acknowledge that guided imagery isn't universally effective. Patients who have a vested interest in maintaining their symptoms, such as those involved in ongoing legal cases, may not respond as well to the technique. This reminds us of the complex interplay between psychological and external factors in the healing process.

Adaptability

The flexibility of guided imagery allows it to be tailored to each individual's specific needs and experiences. From crafting imaginary conversations with celebrities to facilitate healing in children to creating poignant final dialogues with lost loved ones, the technique can be molded to suit a vast array of scenarios.

Potential for Reapplication

Some patients find value in revisiting the technique, either to reinforce previous experiences or to address new aspects of ongoing issues. This reusability adds to the long-term value of guided imagery as a therapeutic tool.

Transformative Potential

At its best, guided imagery can catalyze profound shifts in perspective and behavior, potentially altering the course of a patient's life. The dramatic turnarounds we've witnessed in cases like Sara's recovery from a violent attack exemplify this transformative power.

Complementary Approach

While potent on its own, guided imagery often yields the best results when integrated into a comprehensive treatment plan. It's rare for this technique to be used in isolation; rather, it typically complements other therapeutic approaches to provide holistic care.

Continual Professional Growth

As clinicians become more adept with the technique, their ability to facilitate powerful guided imagery sessions often improves markedly. This potential for ongoing skill development adds another dimension to the technique's value in clinical practice.

These considerations collectively paint a picture of guided imagery as a powerful, flexible, and deeply impactful therapeutic tool. Its ability to engage the mind and emotions in uniquely immersive ways opens doors to healing and growth that more traditional approaches might struggle to access. As we look to the future of mental health treatment, guided imagery stands out as a technique worthy of continued exploration, refinement, and application across a broad spectrum of human experiences and challenges.

Chapter Thirteen

21 Guided Imagery Stories: The Power of Imagination in Healing

The following twenty-one case studies illustrate the versatility, power, and occasional limitations of guided imagery in therapeutic settings. Each story offers a unique glimpse into the transformative potential of this technique, spanning a wide range of issues from trauma and grief to physical pain and phobias. As you read through these accounts, you'll witness the profound impact that guided imagery can have on individuals' lives, often creating lasting change in remarkably short periods.

1. Healing from Sexual Trauma (Seventeen-Year-Old Female)

A seventeen-year-old girl, raped at sixteen, underwent a powerful guided imagery session using the "movie theater" technique. In this visualization, she watched the traumatic event unfold on an imaginary screen, allowing her to process the experience from a safe distance. Her current self comforted her younger self, and she expressed her feelings to the perpetrator. With the support of her higher power, she found the strength to forgive, understanding that the boy who assaulted her lacked appropriate skills to express his feelings.

The session integrated her sixteen-year-old self with her current self, leading to a sense of completion regarding the rape. In subsequent sessions, she used imagery to reconstruct her spiritual, personal, and career life, crafting a new plan for a fresh start in a different environment.

Conclusion

This case demonstrates the potency of guided imagery in processing severe trauma. By providing a safe space to confront and reframe the experience, the technique enabled rapid healing and empowered the patient to move forward positively. The success reported by both the patient and her mother underscores the transformative potential of this approach in treating sexual trauma.

2. Grief Resolution (Louise, Early Sixties)

Louise, a patient in her early sixties, engaged in a guided imagery session to say goodbye to her son, who had died from a drug overdose at age nineteen. During the visualization, she listened to her son express appreciation and gratitude. He conveyed that he was happy and well in the afterlife, aligning with her faith beliefs. This experience allowed Louise to find relief in letting go of her son and cease worrying about him.

Conclusion

This case illustrates the power of guided imagery in facilitating grief resolution, particularly when aligned with the patient's spiritual beliefs. Her immediate positive response ("Wow!") and the subsequent report of peace and closure demonstrate how this technique can provide comfort and acceptance in the face of profound loss. The lack of need for follow-up in the ensuing five years suggests a lasting impact from a single, well-executed session.

3. Pain Management (Riley, Fifty-Six-Year-Old Female)

Riley, a fifty-six-year-old woman experiencing foot pain due to a medical condition, underwent a guided imagery session aimed at pain reduction. The technique incorporated her higher power, Jesus, in a healing meditation. Riley reported feeling deeply relaxed and pain-free following the session.

Conclusion

This case highlights the potential of guided imagery as a tool for pain management. While not intended as a cure or long-term solution, the technique provided immediate relief and equipped the patient with a valuable coping mechanism. This approach can be particularly beneficial for individuals seeking non-pharmacological methods of pain control, offering them a sense of agency in managing their symptoms.

4. Healing Childhood Wounds (Riley, Follow-Up)

In a follow-up session, Riley addressed memories of her father kicking her out as a teenager, which had left her feeling ashamed and inadequate. Using guided imagery, she encountered Jesus, experiencing a profound sense of love and acceptance. This vision reminded her that she wasn't judged or abandoned for her imperfections.

Conclusion

This case demonstrates how guided imagery can be effectively used to heal deep-seated emotional wounds from childhood. By incorporating the patient's spiritual beliefs, the technique facilitated a powerful experience of unconditional love and acceptance. This approach not only addressed the specific traumatic memory but also provided a new, positive framework for self-perception, potentially impacting various aspects of the patient's life.

5. Unresolved Grief (Sixty-Three-Year-Old Male)

A sixty-three-year-old man, grieving the loss of his son in a car accident, approached guided imagery with anxiety. Despite his familiarity with visualization techniques, he struggled to relax during the session and reported feeling unworthy of forgiveness. Both therapist and patient agreed to postpone further attempts until after addressing his self-worth issues.

Conclusion

This case serves as a crucial reminder of the importance of proper preparation before engaging in guided imagery. It illustrates that even individuals comfortable with visualization may face emotional barriers that hinder the effectiveness of the technique. This experience underscores the need for therapists to assess and address underlying issues, such as feelings of unworthiness, before proceeding with guided imagery for grief resolution.

6. Resolving Parental Issues (Lucy)

Lucy, struggling with a critical mother and distant father, engaged in two guided imagery sessions. The first focused on expressing her feelings to her mother at age thirteen. Initially rigid and intellectualized, the session became emotionally charged when integrating her younger self with her current self. In the second session, she addressed her relationship with her father, surprising herself with the depth of emotion she experienced.

Conclusion

This case illustrates the power of guided imagery in resolving complex parental relationships. The technique allowed Lucy to access and process deep-seated emotions, leading to a sense of empowerment and freedom from depression. The lasting positive effects, noted years later, highlight the potential for guided imagery to create enduring change in how individuals perceive and interact with their personal histories.

7. Overcoming Traumatic Mental Imagery (Renee)

Renee had been plagued by a self-created mental image of her husband molesting his teenage daughter, a scenario he had admitted to her. This distressing visualization had haunted her for twenty-five years, driving her to use alcohol as a sleep aid. Through guided imagery, Renee was able to "put away" this tormenting mental movie.

Conclusion

This case demonstrates the effectiveness of guided imagery in addressing intrusive, traumatic mental images. By providing a structured way to confront and dispel the distressing visualization, the technique helped Renee break free from a long-standing pattern of psychological torment and substance abuse. While follow-up was limited due to relocation, the initial positive outcome suggests the potential for guided imagery to disrupt entrenched negative thought patterns and behaviors.

8. Grief Work (Penelope, Seventy-Three-Year-Old Woman)

Penelope, a seventy-three-year-old woman, used guided imagery to say goodbye to her son who had died many years earlier. During the session, she apologized for perceived failings and received forgiveness from her son. Penelope reported feeling significantly better about the situation following the procedure.

Conclusion

This case highlights the enduring nature of grief and the potential for guided imagery to facilitate healing even years after a loss. The mutual exchange of apology and forgiveness during the imagery session provided Penelope with a sense of resolution that had eluded her for years. The lasting effect of this intervention, evidenced by her continued peace with her son's death six years later, when I saw her again for a new issue, underscores the profound and durable impact that a well-executed guided imagery session can have on unresolved grief.

9. Multiple Loss Processing (Samantha)

Samantha, having lost two sons—one to heart disease stemming from drug abuse and another to suicide—engaged in a guided imagery session to address her profound grief. In the visualization, she met with each son individually, hearing their love and gratitude. Guided by her faith, she was able to release them to Jesus, finding comfort in the belief that they were well cared for.

Conclusion

This poignant case illustrates the capacity of guided imagery to address multiple devastating losses simultaneously. By incorporating the patient's spiritual beliefs, the technique provided a framework for acceptance and peace. The powerful, repeated description of the experience and the subsequent shift in focus demonstrate how guided imagery can facilitate a significant emotional breakthrough, allowing individuals to process complex grief and move forward in their healing journey.

10. Saying Goodbye (Joanne)

Joanne participated in a guided imagery session to say a final goodbye to her deceased daughter. She created a mental space where she could see and interact with her daughter one last time. Joanne reported that the experience felt very real and powerful, allowing her to embrace her daughter and express unspoken sentiments.

Conclusion

This case exemplifies how guided imagery can provide a tangible sense of closure in bereavement. By creating a vivid, multisensory experience of saying goodbye, the technique offered Joanne a chance to fulfill her need for a final interaction with her daughter. The reported feelings of hope and closure, coupled with the comfort of anticipating a future reunion, demonstrate how guided imagery can transform the grief process, providing solace and a positive perspective on loss.

11. Processing Childhood Tragedy (Sandra, Sixty-Two-Year-Old)

Sandra, a sixty-two-year-old woman, used guided imagery to address the loss of her two sons who had drowned in her backyard twenty years prior. The imagery took place at the

St. Louis Zoo, where she envisioned her sons in sailor outfits. They communicated their happiness and peace, while also expressing that they missed their parents. The emotional session concluded with Sandra releasing her children.

Conclusion

This case underscores the power of guided imagery in processing long-held grief, even decades after the loss. By creating a specific, emotionally resonant scenario, the technique allowed Sandra to interact with her lost children in a way that provided comfort and closure. The success of the session, evidenced by the reported peace and the lack of need for follow-up, illustrates how a single, well-crafted guided imagery experience can facilitate significant emotional healing for enduring traumatic losses.

12. Phobia Treatment (Ruth, Seventy-Six-Year-Old Female)

Ruth, a seventy-six-year-old woman with a phobia of dying, underwent a guided imagery session that transported her to Sanibel Island Beach, Florida. There, she confronted her fear of death, visualizing it as a tangible object. A comforting being reminded her of the universality of death and assured her of her safety. This allowed Ruth to release her fear, watching it dissipate into the atmosphere.

Conclusion

This case demonstrates the efficacy of guided imagery in addressing deep-seated phobias, particularly those related to existential fears. By providing a safe, controlled environment to confront and reframe her fear of death, the technique enabled Ruth to achieve a significant shift in perspective. The reported changes in her perception of colors and her sense of relief indicate a profound psychological transformation. The continued improvement in her outlook on dying, maintained through monthly treatment, highlights the lasting impact of this guided imagery intervention.

13. Self-Esteem Building (Paolo, Male in Seventies)

Paolo, a man in his seventies, used guided imagery to address feelings of inadequacy stemming from childhood experiences, including humiliation by a Little League coach and bullying. In one session, an older version of Paolo affirmed and demonstrated love to his younger self. In a subsequent session, Paolo used imagery to communicate with his older brother, reflecting on their different personalities.

Conclusion

This case illustrates the versatility of guided imagery in addressing various aspects of self-esteem and relationship issues. The technique allowed Paolo to provide his younger self with the support and love he needed, potentially rewriting his emotional narrative. The success of these sessions, leading to real-life reconnection with his brother, demonstrates how insights gained through guided imagery can translate into tangible improvements in relationships and self-perception.

14. Processing Suicide of Loved One (Martha, Fifty-Six-Year-Old Female)

Martha, a fifty-six-year-old woman, engaged in a guided imagery session to address unresolved issues with her late boyfriend, who had died by suicide four years earlier. The visualization allowed her to say what she needed to say and hear an apology from him. Martha described the experience as incredibly powerful and realistic, noting she could touch him and perceive sensory details like his leather jacket.

Conclusion

This case powerfully demonstrates the potential of guided imagery to facilitate healing in the aftermath of a loved one's suicide. By creating a vivid, multisensory experience, the technique allowed Martha to have the interaction she needed for closure. The immediate impact of this session, evidenced by her ability to move forward in a new relationship, underscores the transformative potential of guided imagery in processing complex grief and guilt associated with suicide loss.

15. Overcoming Driving Anxiety (Amanda, Forty-Six-Year-Old Female)

Amanda, a forty-six-year-old woman unable to drive due to a car accident, underwent a guided imagery session via telehealth. The session involved relaxation on an imaginary beach, followed by watching her accident in a movie theater. Her current self then entered the scene to provide reassurance to her past self. The session concluded with destroying the mental DVD of the accident and replacing it with confidence and gratitude.

Conclusion

This case showcases the adaptability of guided imagery, demonstrating its effectiveness even in a telehealth setting. The technique successfully addressed Amanda's driving anxiety by allowing her to process the traumatic event from a safe distance and then reframe it positively. The reported loss of driving dread and reduction in generalized anxiety highlight the profound impact of this intervention. The lasting effects, noted three and a half years later, underscore the potential for guided imagery to create enduring changes in behavior and emotional responses.

16. Spiritual Healing (Male Patient in Early Seventies)

A man in his early seventies, aspiring to write a book but facing internal blocks, engaged in a guided imagery session. He entered an imaginary room where he confronted his past mistakes and hurts. Through a spiritual experience involving Jesus, he received forgiveness and love, transforming the room into a warm, peaceful space.

Conclusion

This case illustrates the powerful intersection of guided imagery and spiritual beliefs in facilitating emotional healing and personal growth. By creating a vivid scenario aligned with the patient's faith, the technique provided a profound experience of forgiveness and self-acceptance. The intense emotional response and the patient's assertion that he had never experienced anything like it before underscore the transformative potential of guided imagery when it resonates deeply with an individual's belief system and emotional needs.

17. Processing Complicated Grief (Patricia, Female in Mid-Seventies)

Patricia, a woman in her mid-seventies, used guided imagery to address unresolved feelings about her deceased husband, who had been unfaithful. The imagery took place on the island of Kauai, Hawaii, the location of a pleasant memory. Patricia was able to say goodbye to her husband after hearing his expressions of guilt, regret, gratitude, and love.

Conclusion

This case demonstrates the effectiveness of guided imagery in processing complicated grief, particularly when the relationship was marked by betrayal. By choosing a positive setting from their shared history, the technique created a safe space for Patricia to confront and resolve her complex emotions. The ability to forgive and acknowledge that she would miss her husband more now indicates a significant shift in her emotional landscape. This case highlights how guided imagery can facilitate the delicate balance of acknowledging past hurts while allowing for resolution and a new perspective on the relationship.

18. Unresolved Grief in Ongoing Legal Case (Female in Fifties)

A woman in her fifties, who lost her sister in a mass shooting, participated in a guided imagery session (see Chapter Eleven). While she was able to express her sadness, she didn't fully let go of her sister. This was likely due to her ongoing involvement in a lawsuit and her commitment to advocating for policy changes.

Conclusion

This case provides an important lesson about timing and readiness for guided imagery interventions. While the technique allowed for some emotional expression, it did not lead to full resolution. This outcome highlights the complex interplay between grief, ongoing legal processes, and personal advocacy. It serves as a reminder that external factors and personal readiness play crucial roles in the effectiveness of guided imagery, and that it's sometimes necessary to address practical and legal matters before full emotional processing can occur.

19. Parent-Child Reconciliation (Harold, Man in Sixties)

Harold, a man in his sixties, used guided imagery to address the loss of his son to a drug overdose. In the visualization, he was able to make peace with his son, experiencing mutual forgiveness for past imperfections. Harold reported a profound physical sensation following the session, describing it as a pleasant feeling resonating throughout his body.

Conclusion

This case illustrates the power of guided imagery in facilitating posthumous reconciliation and mutual forgiveness. The vivid, emotional nature of the experience, coupled with the reported physical sensations, suggests a deep level of processing and release. The lasting impact of this single session, with effects still notable seven years later, underscores the potential for guided imagery to create enduring emotional resolution, even in cases of profound loss complicated by difficult circumstances.

20. Domestic Violence Trauma (Leslie, Woman in Forties)

Leslie, a woman in her forties, used guided imagery to address a traumatic memory of physical assault by her ex-husband. The session focused on putting away the distressing scene and reclaiming her personal power. Initially, Leslie reported the technique as powerful and helpful.

Conclusion

This case initially demonstrates the effectiveness of guided imagery in processing traumatic memories related to domestic violence. The reported sense of empowerment suggests that the technique successfully helped Leslie reframe her experience and regain a sense of control. However, the need for a "refresher" session years later, triggered by her ex-husband's involvement in their adult child's wedding, highlights an important aspect of trauma recovery: the potential for regression when faced with powerful reminders of past abuse.

This case underscores several key points:

1. The initial success of guided imagery in addressing trauma, providing immediate relief and a sense of empowerment.

2. The potential for long-lasting effects, as evidenced by the seven-year period of improvement.

3. The reality that trauma recovery is often an ongoing process, particularly when dealing with complex interpersonal traumas like domestic violence.

4. The value of guided imagery as a tool that can be revisited when needed, providing a familiar and effective method for restabilization when triggers arise.

5. The importance of follow-up and the potential need for periodic "booster" sessions in some cases, especially when dealing with trauma related to individuals who may still play a role in the patient's life.

Leslie's case serves as a reminder that while guided imagery can be a powerful tool for trauma resolution, it may need to be part of a broader, ongoing strategy for managing the long-term effects of domestic violence. It also highlights the technique's flexibility and repeatability, offering a way for patients to reconnect with their inner resources and coping strategies when faced with unexpected triggers or life events that reactivate old traumas.

21. Childhood Sexual Trauma Resolution (Rick, Sixty-Three-Year-Old Male)

Rick, a sixty-three-year-old radiologist struggling with alcohol addiction, sought therapy after the 2011 Penn State scandal triggered intense flashbacks and nightmares. These disturbing episodes stemmed from a traumatic experience in his middle school years involving a traveling magician.

At age twelve, Rick volunteered for a magic trick during a school performance, feeling proud and excited. The magician invited him backstage afterward, ostensibly to reveal the trick's secret. Instead, Rick fell victim to a horrific sexual assault. The magician threatened to kill Rick's entire family if he ever disclosed the abuse, leaving Rick terrified and silent for fifty-one years.

Using the guided imagery technique, we revisited the entire traumatic event. Rick watched the scene unfold from the safety of an imaginary movie theater, from his initial excitement in the school auditorium to the painful aftermath of the assault. After reviewing every detail, Rick's adult self entered the scene to comfort and encourage his younger self, affirming that the abuse wasn't his fault and that he could finally let go of the burden.

The session was intensely emotional, with Rick spending considerable time sobbing on the couch as he imagined comforting his younger self. We concluded by visualizing Rick destroying the "movie" in an alley behind the theater, symbolically freeing himself from the need to revisit the trauma.

Two weeks later, Rick described the experience. "It was the second worst forty-five minutes of my life [repeating the rape story], followed by the best fifteen minutes of my life [the time spent with Young Rick]." He felt his mind was finally free.

In a powerful gesture, Rick later presented me with a copy of Michelangelo's "Rebellious Slave," depicting a shackled figure breaking free from bondage. Rick said, "This is what you have done for me. I am finally out of bondage."

Conclusion

This case powerfully illustrates the potential of guided imagery in resolving deeply buried childhood trauma. By providing a safe, controlled environment to revisit and reframe the traumatic event, the technique allowed Rick to process his experience and offer comfort to his younger self. The immediate emotional catharsis, followed by a sense of freedom and empowerment, demonstrates the profound healing potential of this approach. Moreover, the subsequent positive life changes—joining AA and maintaining sobriety for over five years—underscore the far-reaching impact of resolving core trauma through guided imagery. This case serves as a testament to the technique's ability to facilitate healing even decades after a traumatic event, potentially transforming not just the specific memory but the overall trajectory of a patient's life.

References

Ackerman, C. E. (2023, May 19). Guided imagery: How to and benefits of visualization techniques. PositivePsychology. com. positivepsychology.com/guided-imagery

Allami, N., Paulignan, Y., Brovelli, A., & Boussaoud, D. (2014). Effects of physical and mental practice on the learning of a target task. *Experimental Brain Research*, 232(1), 183–193.

Beauchamp, M. R., Bray, S. R., & Albinson, J. G. (2017). Imagery use in sport: Mediational effects for efficacy. *Journal of Sports Sciences*, 35(19), 1988–1995.

Beck, B. D., Messel, C., Meyer, S. L., Cordtz, T. O., Søgaard, U., Simonsen, E., & Moe, T. (2017). Feasibility of trauma-focused guided imagery and music with adult refugees diagnosed with PTSD: A pilot study. *Nordic Journal of Music Therapy*, 27(1), 67–86. doi.org/10.1080/08098131.2017.1286368

Bigham, E., McDannel, L., Luciano, I., & Salgado-Lopez, G. (2014). Effect of a brief guided imagery on stress. *Biofeedback*, 42(1), 28–35. doi.org/10.5298/1081-5937-42.1.07

Brewin, C. R. (2015). Re-experiencing traumatic events in PTSD: New avenues in research on intrusive memories and flashbacks. *European Journal of Psychotraumatology*, 6(1). doi.org/10.3402/ejpt.v6.27180

Capuzzi, D., & Stauffer, M. D. (2022). *Counseling and Psychotherapy: Theories and Interventions*. American Counseling Association.

Cortman, C., & Shinitzky, H. E. (2009). *Your Mind: An Owner's Manual for a Better Life*. Career Press.

Cortman, C., & Walden, J. (2018). *Keep Pain in the Past: Getting Over Trauma, Grief, and the Worst That's Ever Happened to You*. Mango.

Cortman, C., Shinitzky, H., & O'Connor, R. (2014). *Take Control of Your Anxiety: A Drug-Free Approach to Living a Happy, Healthy Life*. Career Press.

Cupal, D. D., & Brewer, B. W. (2004). Effects of relaxation and guided imagery on knee strength, reinjury anxiety, and pain following anterior cruciate ligament reconstruction. *Rehabilitation Psychology*, 49(2), 91–101.

Feltz, D. L., & Landers, D. M. (1991). The effects of mental practice on motor skill learning and performance: A meta-analysis. *Journal of Sport Psychology*, 5(1), 25–57.

Frank, C., Land, W. M., Popp, C., & Schack, T. (2013). The effect of combined mental and physical practice on the learning of a discrete motor skill. *Mental Imagery in Motor Learning and Performance*, 18(1), 67–82.

Gardner, R. A. (1992). *The Parental Alienation Syndrome: A Guide for Mental Health and Legal Professionals*. Creative Therapeutics.

Giacobbi Jr., P. R., Dreisbach, K. A., Thurlow, N. M., Anand, P., & Garcia, F. (2011). The use of mental imagery to enhance intrinsic motivation. *Journal of Sport and Exercise Psychology*, 33(3), 416–433.

Hale, B. D., & Whitehouse, A. (2002). The effect of guided imagery practice on competitive anxiety in young elite athletes. *Journal of Applied Sport Psychology*, 14(2), 149–161.

Hall, C. R., Mack, D. E., Paivio, A., & Hausenblas, H. A. (1998). Imagery use by athletes: Development of the Sport Imagery Questionnaire. *International Journal of Sport Psychology*, 29(1), 73–89.

Highstein, M. (2013, June 16). History of guided imagery. Guided Imagery Downloads. guidedimagerydownloads.com/history-of-guided-imagery

Holmes, T. H., & Rahe, R. H. (1967). The social readjustment rating scale. *Journal of Psychosomatic Research*, 11(2), 213–218. doi.org/10.1016/0022-3999(67)90010-4

Hutton, D. (2023, September 8). Expert untangles complexities of grief for suicide loss survivors. CU Anschutz News. news.cuanschutz.edu/news-stories/expert-untangles-complexities-of-grief-for-suicide-loss-survivors

King, K. (2010). A review of the effects of guided imagery on cancer patients with pain. *Complementary Health Practice Review*, 15(2), 98–107. doi.org/10.1177/1533210110388113

Kolata, G. (2014, February 22). Olympians use imagery as mental training. *The New York Times.* nytimes. com/2014/02/23/sports/olympics/olympians-use-imagery-as-mental-training.html

Kovach, A. M. S. (1985). Shamanism and guided imagery and music: A comparison. *Journal of Music Therapy,* 22(3), 154–165.

Krau, S. D. (2020). The multiple uses of guided imagery. *Nursing Clinics of North America,* 55(4), 467–474. doi. org/10.1016/j.cnur.2020.06.013

Kushner, H. S. (1981). *When Bad Things Happen to Good People.* Schocken Books.

Lee, N. B. (2018). Re-experiencing the past through the Bonny method of guided imagery and music: music imagery, emotional memory, and the brain. *Journal of the Association for Music and Imagery,* 45–75. doi.org/10.59451/jami.53356

Leuner, H. (1978). Basic principles and therapeutic efficacy of guided affective imagery (GAI). *The Power of Human Imagination,* 125–166. doi.org/10.1007/978-1-4613-3941-0_5

Markland, D., Hall, C. R., Duncan, L. R., & Simatovic, J. (2015). The effects of an imagery intervention on implicit and explicit exercise attitudes. *Psychology of Sport and Exercise,* 17, 24–31.

Martin, D. G. (2016). *Counseling and Therapy Skills.* Waveland Press.

McLeod, S. (2023). Self-efficacy and social cognitive theories. Simply Psychology. simplypsychology.org/self-efficacy.html

Munroe, K. J., Giacobbi Jr, P. R., Hall, C., & Weinberg, R. (1998). The use of imagery by athletes in selected sports. *The Sport Psychologist, 12*(4), 440–449.

National Institute of Mental Health. (2022, September). Major depression. nimh.nih.gov/health/statistics/major-depression

Pepper, S. C. (1942). *World Hypotheses: A Study in Evidence.* University of California Press.

Perls, F. S., Hefferline, R. F., & Goodman, P. (1994). *Gestalt Therapy: Excitement and Growth in the Human Personality.* Gestalt Journal.

Perls, F. S., & Wysong, J. (1992). *Gestalt Therapy Verbatim.* Gestalt Journal.

Pirsig, R. M. (n.d.). Robert M. Pirsig quotes. The Quotations Page. quotationspage.com/quote/31469.html

Post, P. G., Wrisberg, C. A., & Mullins, S. (2012). The effect of mental imagery with specific verbal cues on field goal kicking performance. *The Sport Psychologist, 26*(4), 645–658.

Ramsey, R., Cumming, J., Edwards, M. G., Williams, S., & Brunning, C. (2009). Effects of PETTLEP imagery on netball shooting performance. *Journal of Sport and Exercise Psychology, 31*, S97-S97.

Roberts, C. (2019, January 14). What is guided imagery? The ultimate guide. Calm Chronicles. generationcalm.com/blog/what-is-guided-imagery-the-ultimate-guide

Roffe, L., Schmidt, K., & Ernst, E. (2005). A systematic review of guided imagery as an adjuvant cancer therapy. *Psycho-Oncology*, 14(8), 607–617. doi.org/10.1002/pon.889

Rossman, M. (2000). *Guided Imagery for Self-Healing: An Essential Resource*. H. J. Kramer.

Rubel, B. (n.d.). Guided imagery when there's unfinished business. Griefwork Center. griefworkcenter.com/guided-imagery-when-theres-unfinished-business

Schultz, D. P., & Schultz, S. E. (2017). *Theories of Personality*. Cengage.

Shahbazi, M., & Tahmasebi, S. (2007). The effect of mental imagery on the performance of vertical jump. *Research in Sport Science*, 5(15), 93–107.

Shiromani, P. J., Keane, T. M., & LeDoux, J. E. (2009). *Post-Traumatic Stress Disorder: Basic Science and Clinical Practice*. Humana.

Sports Insights. (2022, July 25). Examining NFL key numbers for over/unders. sportsinsights.com/blog/examining-nfl-key-numbers-overunders

Trakhtenberg, E. C. (2008). The effects of guided imagery on the immune system: A critical review. *International Journal of Neuroscience*, 118(6), 839–855. doi.org/10.1080/00207450701792705

Utay, J., & Miller, M. (2006). Guided imagery as an effective therapeutic technique: A brief review of its history and efficacy research. *Journal of Instructional Psychology*, 33(1), 40–43.

Vanzin, L., & Mauri, V. (2020). *Understanding Conduct Disorder and Oppositional-Defiant Disorder: A Guide to Symptoms, Management and Treatment*. Routledge.

Woolfolk, R. L., Parrish, M. W., & Murphy, S. M. (1993). Effects of imagery training on swimming performance: An applied study. *Imagination, Cognition and Personality*, 13(2), 153–166.

World Health Organization. (2024, January 10). Post-traumatic stress disorder. who.int/news-room/fact-sheets/detail/post-traumatic-stress-disorder

Wright, C. J., & Smith, D. (2016). The effects of PETTLEP imagery on strength performance. *International Journal of Sport and Exercise Psychology*, 14(3), 269–280.

Acknowledgements

In bringing this work to fruition, I am deeply indebted to several people whose contributions have been invaluable. First, I wish to express my profound gratitude to Dr. Roger Davis, whose expertise as a psychologist, boundless knowledge, and sharp editorial eye have greatly enhanced this work. His wisdom and guidance have been instrumental in shaping these pages.

I owe a special debt of gratitude to Brenda Knight, who has been an invaluable bridge to Books That Save Lives. Her role as both facilitator and advocate has been crucial in establishing and nurturing my relationship with this wonderful publishing company. Her encouragement and dedicated representation have made this publishing journey both possible and pleasurable.

I am especially grateful to all my patients who have trusted me to guide them through their healing journeys using guided imagery. Their courage, trust, and unwavering determination to achieve wellness have not only made this work possible, but have also taught me countless lessons along the way. Their experiences and successes are the heart of this book.

Finally, my deepest appreciation goes to my wife and office manager, Amanda. Her tireless dedication, from countless hours of proofreading to masterful handling of administrative tasks, has been the backbone of this project. Her technological expertise, far surpassing my own, has been instrumental in bringing this work to completion. But beyond her professional contributions, it is her unwavering love, support, and encouragement that have sustained me throughout this journey. Her beauty, both inside and out, continues to inspire me daily. Her presence in my life is truly priceless, and I am profoundly grateful for her partnership in both life and work.

About the Author

Dr. Christopher Cortman has facilitated over 80,000 hours of psychotherapy during his distinguished career spanning more than three decades. A Florida-licensed psychologist since 1985, he maintains a thriving private practice while specializing in emotional trauma, relationship issues, depression, and anxiety disorders.

Named "Best Psychologist" for ten consecutive years by readers of the *Venice Gondolier Sun* and recipient of Florida's "Outstanding Contributions to Psychology in the Public Interest" award, Dr. Cortman is a sought-after expert who has appeared on Disney Radio, MTV, and ABC. He has shared speaking platforms with prominent figures including Tipper Gore, Jane Pauley, and Patrick Kennedy, addressing mental health stigma through his signature "edu-tainment" approach that combines clinical expertise with engaging humor.

Dr. Cortman is the creator of the Social Black Belt program and the acclaimed author of five books, including *Your Mind: An Owner's Manual for a Better Life*, *Take Control of Your Anxiety*, and *Keep Pain in the Past*. He holds a doctorate in psychology from ISIU (now Alliant) in San Diego and continues to pioneer innovative approaches to mental health education and treatment.

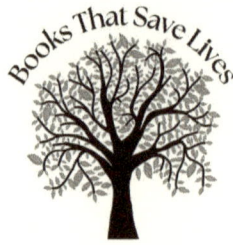

Books That Save Lives

About the Publisher

Books That Save Lives came into being in 2024 when the editor and publisher, Brenda Knight, heard directly from readers and authors that certain self-help, grief, psychology books, and journals were providing a lifeline for folks. We live in a stressful world where it is increasingly difficult not to feel overwhelmed, worried, depressed, and downright scared. We intend to offer support for the vulnerable, including people struggling with mental wellness and physical illness as well as people of color, queer and trans adults and teens, immigrants and anyone who needs encouragement and inspiration.

From first responders, military veterans, and retirees to LGBTQ+ teens and to those experiencing the shock of bereavement and loss, our books have saved lives. To us, there is no higher calling.

We would love to hear from you! Our readers are our most important resource; we value your input, suggestions, and ideas.

Please stay in touch with us and follow us at:

www.booksthatsavelives.net

https://www.instagram.com/booksthatsavelives/

www.ingramcontent.com/pod-product-compliance
Lightning Source LLC
Chambersburg PA
CBHW021136090426
42740CB00008B/810